The Power of Your Personal Impact

STAN TOLER

HARVEST HOUSE PUBLISHERS
EUGENE, OREGON

Cover by Kyler Dougherty

Cover image © letoosen / Gettyimages

For bulk, special sales, or ministry purchases, please call 1-800-547-8979.
Email: customerservice@hhp.books.com

M is a federally registered trademark of The Hawkins Children's LLC. Harvest House Publishers, Inc., is the exclusive licensee of the trademark.

The Power of Your Personal Impact

Copyright © 2018 Stan Toler
Published by Harvest House Publishers
Eugene, Oregon 97408
www.harvesthousepublishers.com

ISBN: 978-0-7369-8239-9 (pbk.)
ISBN: 978-0-7369-8240-5 (eBook)

The Library of Congress has cataloged the edition as follows:

Names: Toler, Stan, author.
Title: The power of your influence : 11 ways to make a difference in your
    world / Stan Toler.
Description: Eugene, Oregon : Harvest House Publishers, 2018.
Identifiers: LCCN 2017046610 (print) | LCCN 2017061156 (ebook) | ISBN
    9780736973069 (ebook) | ISBN 9780736973052 (pbk.)
Subjects: LCSH: Influence (Psychology)—Religious aspects—Christianity. |
    Power (Christian theology) | Change—Religious aspects—Christianity.
Classification: LCC BV4597.53.I52 (ebook) | LCC BV4597.53.I52 T65 2018
    (print) | DDC 248.4—dc23
LC record available at https://lccn.loc.gov/2017046610

Printed in the United States of America

21 22 23 24 25 26 27 28 29 / BP-CD / 10 9 8 7 6 5 4 3 2 1

CONTENTS

THE POWER TO CHANGE THE FUTURE

What is leadership? It's an influence process—any time you are trying to influence the thinking, behavior, or development of another, you are engaging in leadership.

KEN BLANCHARD[1]

Y ou're reading this book because you want to change the world. Perhaps you wouldn't state it quite so dramatically, but the reason you picked up a book on the power of influence is that you have a vision for your life—or your family, community, church, or country—that remains unfulfilled. You want something to be different tomorrow than it is today.

Maybe that something is as mundane as having a clean house. You'd like your family or your roommates to pick up after themselves and do the dishes occasionally. You're tired of nagging, and you don't know what to do next.

Or perhaps you are after larger-scale change. You'd like to change the culture in your workplace or see different policies enacted at your school. You may even aspire to end human trafficking or solve the clean-water crisis in a developing country.

Whatever your dream may be, you've probably already discovered two important things: (1) You cannot achieve this alone, and (2) you cannot force others to join you. The only way to bring real, lasting change to your world is to harness the single most powerful attribute that you or any human being possesses: influence.

METHODS THAT DON'T WORK

When people long for change, they normally begin by trying two things that are equally ineffective. No doubt you've traveled these roads already. The first is to try to change the world by working harder. We might call this the *power-of-one* method.

The Power-of-One Method

When you see a problem, you say to yourself, "I can do something about this!" And you dive in with all your energy. You notice the trash along the roadside in your neighborhood, so you stop and pick it up. You want your organization to be more effective and efficient, so you stay later to get more done. You want the world to be a better place, so you become a better person.

The power-of-one approach is well illustrated by the often-repeated story of the starfish.[2] According to one variation of the story, a young man is walking along the beach when he notices an older man picking up starfish that have been stranded by the tide and, one by one, throwing them back into the sea. The younger man surveys the beach and sees a countless multitude of helpless creatures on the sand.

"Look at all these starfish," he says to the old man. "There must be thousands of them. What difference do you think you can make saving one starfish at a time?"

The old man nods, then picks up a starfish, throws it back into the water, and says, "It made a great difference for that one."

The story illustrates the impact one individual can have on another, and it's inspiring at that level. Yet many people who apply this philosophy eventually become frustrated and discouraged. They are moved by a great need but quickly become overwhelmed by its scope. Saving one starfish doesn't solve the underlying problem, so they work harder and harder and harder. At the end of the day—or a few weeks, or perhaps a year or two—they become exhausted, crushed by the weight of an endless need. Some professions have developed terms to describe this, like *burnout* and *compassion fatigue.*

Working harder will not eliminate the problems you dream of solving. You will only exhaust yourself in the process. And that brings us to a second, equally futile approach.

The Power-Up Method

Realizing that the power of one will never be enough, many well-intentioned folks aim to enlist others in achieving the change they hope for. But, as you may have noticed, other people don't always do what we'd like them to do. When they don't, our first resort is often to apply some form of pressure to gain their compliance. We might call this the *power-up* approach.

We discipline our children, sometimes using corporal punishment, to make them behave. We implement policies in the workplace that will compel others to comply. We even pass laws that will force others to behave as we think they should. And those are just the formal uses of the power-up approach. Informally, we may resort to manipulation, social pressure, or even threats and intimidation to make others join us in the wonderful world we are trying to create.

The power-up approach is doomed to fail, however. Though it may be successful in the short term, social scientists have found that punishment is simply ineffective in changing behavior permanently.[3] When the punishment or other external pressure is removed, people immediately revert to their former ways. And there are many occasions when powering up simply backfires, causing others to harden in their resolve.

Perhaps the best recent example of this comes from the Civil Rights Movement. During the early 1960s, civil-rights activists sought to desegregate bus terminals, universities, restrooms, and other public accommodations in accordance with federal law. Those in positions of authority powered up to prevent it. Activists were met with firm, often violent, resistance, including frequent arrests and the use of fire hoses and attack dogs. Those power tactics backfired, however, as activists persevered and continued to take their stand. In time, public sympathy swung in their favor.

Power tactics may bring a temporary change to a given situation, but they never work in the long run. To achieve the changes you envision, nagging, arguing, intimidating, or even legislating will not change the hearts and minds of others. To do that, you need a tool that is far more subtle, powerful, and effective. You need the power of influence.

A BETTER WAY

On August 28, 1963, Dr. Martin Luther King Jr. stood on the steps of the Lincoln Memorial in Washington, D.C., and addressed a crowd of some 250,000 people. As you may know, King was the leader of a nonviolent resistance movement aimed at securing equal rights for persons regardless of race. Rather than powering up, King's followers powered down, allowing themselves to be arrested and sometimes beaten without fighting back. On that day in Washington, King delivered his now-famous speech "I Have a Dream," in which he said he looked forward to the day when "all of God's children"—no matter their background—could join hands and proclaim they are "free at last!"[4]

These words rallied millions to the cause of civil rights. Without a bullhorn or bullwhip, nor a fire hose nor an attack dog nor a pair of handcuffs, Dr. King moved millions of people to change their minds about a pressing social issue, and thus changed the character of a nation. How did he do it? With the power of influence.

The purpose of this book is to enable you to achieve your dreams by teaching you to leverage that very power. If you are exhausted from trying to bring about change all by yourself, this book is for you. It will equip you to enlist others in pursuing your vision. If you are frustrated and perhaps even feeling foolish or guilty for the ways you've "powered up" on others, trying to force them to see things your way, this book is for you too. It will help you discover the freedom and confidence to simply be yourself, knowing that your life, your character, and the strength of your vision have far more potential to bring change than does any form of physical power or manipulation. And the stakes are high. Living out your faith by mastering the power of influence is one of the most important things you will ever do.

WHY THIS MATTERS

The power of influence matters so much because without it, you'll be trapped in a cycle of frustration and ineffectiveness. The danger is that you may not achieve the dreams you have for yourself, or you may even find yourself worse off than before. That's what happened at on July 25, 1914. Two days earlier, Baron Giesl von Gieslingen, the ambassador of the Austro-Hungarian Empire to Serbia, handed a note to the Serbian foreign ministry. A Serbian nationalist had assassinated Austrian Archduke Franz Ferdinand and his wife in Sarajevo, Bosnia. In response, the Austro-Hungarians powered up. They insisted the Serbian government comply to certain terms of agreement over the matter.

The Austrians assumed they could easily win with such a power move, but they were wrong. The deadline came and went, and Serbia mobilized its army. Three days later, Austria-Hungary declared war on the Serbs. Other European powers soon joined their allies on either side of the conflict, and World War I had begun, eventually costing more than 17 million lives.

When you resort to power over influence, you can have no idea what the unintended consequences will be. You probably won't start an international war, but using power tactics in your home, your workplace, your church, or your community can have devastating effects. You risk losing relationships, bruising friendships, damaging your marriage, and destroying the very community context you hope to influence.

Gutting it out with the power-of-one approach can be disastrous also. The stress you may accumulate from overworking, over-caring, overcommitting, and overextending yourself can greatly affect your health—both physical and emotional—and your overall well-being.

Perhaps the worst consequence of not understanding the power of your influence is that you may never reach the goals you dream about. Your life, your family, and your community may never change in the ways you envision if you are not able to enlist others to join you through the positive, magnetic, irresistible power of your influence.

POWER FOR GOOD

Perhaps you've heard the old story about the salt shop. A man walked into a store one day and asked if they sold salt. "Sure," the clerk said, "we've got lots of it. What kind do you need?"

"I'm not sure," the man replied. "Why don't you show me what you have."

Taking the customer by the arm, the clerk led him through the store, where he showed him row after row of table salt. "Is this what you're looking for?" the clerk asked.

"I don't think so," the man replied.

"No worries," said the clerk. "Follow me." He led the customer deeper into the store to show shelves of kosher salt, rock salt, Himalayan salt, sea salt, flaked salt, pickling salt, softener salt, smoked salt, Alaea salt, and fleur de sel.

The customer's eyes went wide with wonder. "Oh my!" he exclaimed. "You really do sell salt, don't you?"

"Not really," the clerk replied. "We hardly sell any at all. But that salt salesman, wow! He really knows how to sell salt."

When you master the power of influence, like the salt salesman, you'll unlock your ability to enlist others in following your lead. Without powering up and without working yourself to death, you'll begin to see the changes you envision. But make no mistake, influence is not mere salesmanship. Influence is the effect we have on others through our words, actions, and attitudes. It is the power of your life, character, and vision, shaping your world for the better. Yet most of us are unaware of the impact we have on others—either positive or negative.

What do you want to accomplish? Take a moment and envision the change you hope for in your family, in your community, or in your world. You're about to learn the lessons that will enable you to make this vision a reality.

THE ROAD AHEAD

This book will show you how influence works on yourself, those around you, and the world at large. You will discover the tremendous power you have to affect the world for good, along with practical strategies to leverage that influence in order to make positive change.

Part 1 of this book lays a *cognitive foundation* for what follows. You will come to *understand* the nature of influence and how it operates in your life.

Chapter 1 introduces the idea that *influence is the subtle effect you have on others through your words, actions, and attitudes.* Your influence can be sweet and attractive, like the smell of freshly baked cookies, enticing others to follow. Or it can have precisely the opposite effect. Like the first negative comment on social media, your influence may draw others into negative thinking and actions, leaving them worse off than before. You will become aware of the ways you currently influence others and be motivated to use your influence to make positive change.

Chapter 2 defines the *three dimensions of influence*: self, others, and the world. These are not discrete areas, as if influence in one arena were somehow separate from influence in the others. Rather, these three dimensions operate simultaneously. You have the power to influence your own thoughts and behaviors, the attitudes and actions of others, and those at one remove from you (the world). You will understand the dimensions of influence and realize the importance of influencing yourself and your great potential for influencing others.

Part 2 of the book is about crafting your influence. You will learn the nine key sources of your influence and how to produce a greater influence on others.

Chapter 3 describes the *power of your vision*. Vision is your preferred version of the future, a picture of the positive change you are trying to make in yourself and others. A strong, positive vision brings two benefits. First, it acts as a beacon in your life, guiding each choice you make. Second, it attracts others who may have a vague wish for positive change but have no idea how to articulate or pursue it. A person with a strong faith and a vision for the future will influence others. In this chapter, you will be prompted to articulate the positive change you are trying to make and to organize your life around it.

Chapter 4 describes the *power of your thoughts*. Your thoughts determine your influence because they affect everything about you. You cannot hope to influence others positively until you are thinking and living positively yourself. Centering on the age-old wisdom that "as [a man] thinks in his heart, so is he" (Proverbs 23:7 (NKJV), this chapter describes the incredible power of your thoughts in forming your actions and character. You will learn how to influence your own attitudes and actions by choosing positive patterns of thought.

Chapter 5 describes the *power of your words*. They are the single most powerful means of influence at your disposal. This chapter illustrates the near inevitability that complaining, naysaying, belittling, and other forms of self-fulfilling prophecy will be realized. You will also be shown the tremendous power of positive speech to shape reality, while learning the speech patterns that influence others and gaining practical strategies for harnessing the power of positive speech.

Chapter 6 describes the *power of your example*. Your example is the silent influence you have over others, even when you are not aware of it. By embodying the change you hope to see in the world, you place a seal upon your words, giving them even greater power. In this chapter, you will learn how your example actually influences others, the factors that limit your positive example, and how to cultivate a consistently strong influence through your habits and actions.

Chapter 7 describes the *power of your presence*. Presence is the impact a person makes on others simply by being in the room. Presence is the sum of a number of subtle factors, including demeanor, manner of speech, facial expression, energy level, and behavior. In this chapter, you will come to see the often-underestimated effect of your presence both in person and online, and you will discover strategies for changing "the temperature of the room" simply by being present.

Chapter 8 describes the *power of your encouragement*. Encouragement is a form of positive speech that takes influence to a new level. When you encourage others, you directly influence their thoughts and actions. The results can be astounding. In this chapter, you will discover the explosive power of encouragement and be motivated to practice it consistently in your relationships.

Chapter 9 describes the *power of your generosity*. Generosity is giving to others without expectation or obligation. You can be generous with time, abilities, or resources. Generosity influences others in two ways. First, it establishes leadership by example, showing others the needs or opportunities that are most important. Second, it has a nudge effect, prompting others to be generous also. In this chapter, you will be inspired to become more generous and will be prompted to identify specific ways to practice generosity.

Chapter 10 describes the *power of your commitment*. Commitment is your willingness to stick with a positive vision even when it's difficult to achieve. Strong commitment is highly influential because people respect those who are willing to sacrifice for a goal over the long term. This chapter will provide strong motivation to remain engaged in the process of change over time.

Chapter 11 describes the *power of your sacrifice*. Generosity is sharing from abundance; sacrifice is giving of oneself at a level that risks loss. Sacrifice produces the most powerful influence because it is a demonstration of love. The influence of Gandhi, Dr. Martin Luther King Jr., Billy Graham, Bill Bright, John C. Maxwell, and other great leaders endures precisely because they were willing to put the needs of others ahead of their own. In this chapter, you will be inspired to give the greatest possible gift to others: yourself.

Finally, each chapter concludes with The Key Three: three critical questions for personal reflection. Remember that none of the learning in this book will benefit you if it stays inside your head. To be of use, it must trickle down into your heart and flow out through your words and actions. By reflecting on the ideas communicated here, you will both solidify the learning in your mind and discover practical ways to translate that learning into action.

When we have finished, you will *realize* what influence is, *understand* how it operates in your life and the lives of others, and *be empowered* to extend your influence to make positive change in yourself and in the world around you. What would you like to accomplish today? We're about to begin the journey to achieve that goal.

THE KEY THREE

1. State the main reason you're reading this book. What do you hope to achieve by it?

2. Are you more likely to resort to the power-of-one method, the power-up method, or the power of influence? Why?

3. How would you define *influence*?

Part 1

UNDERSTANDING YOUR PERSONAL IMPACT

THE NATURE OF YOUR PERSONAL IMPACT

Our chief want in life is somebody
who shall make us do what we can.

RALPH WALDO EMERSON[1]

You've heard it said, "There's one in every crowd." Most of the time when that well-worn descriptor of human behavior is used, it's not good news. It is often applied to someone who stands out because of their negative impact on others. "There's one in every crowd" could be applied to the person who always speaks their mind while others stare at the floor or the sky. It could refer to that one person who forgets to turn off their cell phone at church or who drives slow in the passing lane. It might be said of that one guy who yells "Get in the hole!" at a golf tournament, before the golfer has even taken a swing. It seems that in every place people gather, there's one ill-mannered, boorish, or obnoxious person. We've all experienced the negative power of that one person among many. If we're honest, we would probably admit that we've *been* that person on some occasions. The saying "There's one in every crowd" usually refers to negative influence, the power we all have to affect others in destructive ways.

Negative influence is easy to spot because it makes an immediate impression. It's noticeable. Less noticeable—but just as impactful— is "that one person" who exercises a positive influence. Though we haven't coined a phrase to describe this phenomenon, we have all experienced it. I'm talking about that one person who holds the door open for others, setting a tone for politeness in the workplace. Or it could be the one person who arrives home in a good mood, transforming a hectic day into an enjoyable family dinnertime. Or it could be the one person who lightens the mood with a little humor after receiving bad news. Motivational speaker Zig Ziglar said, "Send out a cheerful, positive greeting, and most of the time you will get back a cheerful, positive greeting. It's also true that if you send out a negative greeting, you will, in most cases, get back a negative greeting."[2] That's precisely true, and it describes the tremendous power of influence in our lives. Though these may seem like mundane examples, they are anything but that.

This chapter will define influence and show you how it operates in your life. You will become more aware of the ways you currently influence others, and you will be motivated to use that influence to make positive change. You can be "that one person" who changes the world for the better. Are you ready to try?

THE DEFINITION OF INFLUENCE

Influence is the subtle effect you have on others through your words, actions, and attitudes. Your influence can be sweet and attractive, like the smell of freshly baked cookies, enticing others to follow—or it can have precisely the opposite effect. Like the first negative comment on social media, your influence may draw others into negative thinking and actions, leaving them worse off than before. Let me illustrate this concept with an employment experience shared by my friend Lawrence.

When Lawrence was in college, he worked at a shoe store, where he was one of the leading salesmen. "Being one of the best made me a little cocky," he confessed, "so I got a bit lazy with some of the less-desirable aspects of the job." Lawrence gradually quit putting away the "drags," or unsold shoes shown to customers, and stopped pitching in with store-closing tasks like vacuuming the floor and restocking displays. "I even got a bit sassy to the assistant manager," he admitted, referring to the person who was often assigned the evening shift.

Before long, the power of influence kicked in and other employees followed suit. Within a few weeks, the store became a stressful and chaotic place as other employees also refused to cooperate with the managers. "That's when Charlie brought me in for a little chat," Lawrence said.

Charlie was the store manager, a good-natured guy but nevertheless a strong leader. "Charlie sat me down and started asking questions," Lawrence recounted. "He asked how I was doing. Whether I was having any problems at home or at school. If I was upset or in any kind of trouble. I was a bit taken aback because he seemed so interested in me."

When Lawrence admitted that everything in life was fine, Charlie zeroed in on the real problem. "Then you have no excuse for the way you've been acting," he said. "I'd like you to start pitching in with the extra chores, and treat my assistant with more respect." Then came the real power words: "I expect more from you, Lawrence. You're better than this."

Ouch! Lawrence thought. "I knew he was right," he said. "To be honest, I had no idea how my bad attitude was affecting others, and I didn't want to be 'that guy.' Charlie motivated me to change."

This is the power of influence in action. Every day, your attitudes, words, and actions are operating on those around you. If you are alive, you have influence. The only question is whether that influence will be positive or negative. Will you be "that one guy" who writes a sarcastic comment on every social media post, poisoning the online atmosphere? Or will you be "that one gal" who, like the shoe store manager, influences others to be the best version of themselves? How will you use your influence?

ASPECTS OF INFLUENCE

To take control of your influence, you must understand what it is and how it operates. It's a bit like flying an airplane. Flight is a complex process involving the forces of thrust, lift, and drag, not to mention the added impact of the weather and the aerodynamics of the craft. It would be foolish—and dangerous—to hop into a Cessna with no training and expect to fly. Yet anyone can learn to fly, given proper instruction and a little experience. The same is true of exercising influence. You can lead others in positive ways when you understand these key aspects of influence.

Influence Is Subtle

First, influence is subtle. Though it is the strongest power you possess, it does not always produce an immediate, visible impact. To exert influence is to play the long game, aiming for victory in months or years, or even over a lifetime.

We are conditioned to believe that the effects of exercising power will be immediate, visible, and overwhelming. Possibly that's because we've seen physical power applied that way during wartime. Military terms like *blitzkrieg* and *shock and awe* have made their way into our vocabulary, influencing the way we think about producing change in any area of life, not just the battlefield. We have come to expect immediate results for our efforts.

Living in the digital age probably contributes to this expectation as well. Not that long ago, a computer that took less than five minutes to boot up was considered "fast." We now expect electronic devices to boot on demand and web pages to load instantly. When we press "send," we assume that the other person has already received our text.

Not surprisingly, we bring this expectation of immediate, visible results to our desire for change. We'd like to change a policy at work and see immediate compliance, or explain to our spouse how we feel about an issue and gain instant agreement. When we don't see a direct response to our efforts, we become frustrated. That's when we're tempted to either power up or give up.

Influence, however, does not always produce instant results. Its power is subtle, sometimes almost imperceptible. Yet influence, over the long term, can exert irresistible force. What may begin as a single raindrop of influence can, over time, become an inescapable flood.

In that way, influence is like the power exerted by the moon as compared with the power of the sun. The sun represents direct power. When it shines directly on you, its heat and intensity are impossible to ignore. That's especially true at higher elevations or in places closer to the earth's equator. Stand in direct sunlight in the mountains of Colorado, and your skin will burn in a matter of minutes. Those burning rays will have you putting on a hat or reaching for the sunscreen. Or take a walk in the tropical sun at midday, and you'll very quickly tire from the heat. You'll soon take shelter in the shade until that burning lamp gets a bit lower in the sky.

The sun's power is direct, immediate, and overwhelming. Just what we'd like our influence to be.

In reality, however, our influence is more like the power of the moon. We see the moon far less often because it's visible mostly at night. And the intensity of the moon's glow is only a fraction of the sun's. You can look directly at the moon without shielding your eyes, and nobody ever put on a hat to protect themselves from moon burn.

Yet the moon exerts tremendous power on the earth, moving the tide of vast oceans twice a day. Because the moon is much closer to the earth than is the sun, the moon's gravitational pull is actually greater than that of the massive star. The moon can raise or lower the level of the ocean by several feet, an effect that is amplified closer to shore and in bays or estuaries. In Canada's Bay of Fundy, the tide produces a sea-level change of more than 40 feet. This tidal change is so dramatic that it causes the falls on the Saint John River in New Brunswick to flow backward twice each day!

You could stare at the seashore for hours and not realize that the moon was gently, persistently affecting the level of the ocean. Yet if you didn't move for a long time, you'd get your feet wet.

Just because the influence of the moon is subtle does not mean that it lacks power or effect. The same is true for your influence. You may not see its impact in a day or even a year, but over time your attitudes, words, and actions will produce change in the world around you.

Influence Is Continual

Few things are more annoying than a dripping faucet. A single drop of water has very little power by itself. You probably wouldn't notice the sound, and 0.05 milliliters of H_2O would evaporate very quickly. Yet one drop of water every few seconds quickly becomes a headache, both psychologically and physically. The sound is enough to drive you crazy, and those single drops combined would be enough to soak through the floor in a matter of hours.

Influence, positive or negative, is similar in that no single instance may be decisive. However, hour by hour, day by day, and year by year, the power of our influence adds up. We influence others constantly, whether we are aware of it or not. But those moments of influence are like single drops of water. It is their aggregate force that produces results.

Think of it this way: anyone can arrive for work in either a good mood or a bad mood. If you enter your workplace a bit snarly one time, few people would probably notice. But show up with a scowl day after day, and you'll begin to disrupt the team. Some will start to avoid you. Others will join in the grumpiness or complaining, and the entire environment will be affected by your negative influence.

In the same way, if you compliment a coworker on her performance once, that kind word will be appreciated but could be easily forgotten. However, if you look for opportunities to praise others for a job well done and frequently offer pats on the back, they'll soon look to you for leadership. Your positive attitude will influence others.

The key thing to remember is that you are *always* influencing others, whether you want to or not. Your life is like a radio transmitter. It is always broadcasting a message, whether it's "I'm bored," or "I'm angry," or "This is stupid"—or something more positive like, "I'm in a good mood," or "You're welcome." Your attitude, words, and actions continually exert their gravitational pull on others.

Think about how you spent the last 24 hours. What did you do? What kind of mood were you in? What were you thinking about? Whom did you see, speak to, interact with? And here's the most vital question: Was your influence on those people positive or negative? Were you more like a dripping faucet or a gentle breeze? You influence others whether you choose to or not, so the best thing is to be intentional about exerting a positive influence.

Influence Is Dynamic

There's a documentary that goes by the title "You Can't Be Neutral on a Moving Train."[3] The idea is that the train has picked a direction, even if you haven't. It's impossible to stand still on earth while the train is moving; you're going one direction or another. Your influence is like that. It is dynamic, not static. It will affect others in some way, either positively or negatively.

Some people have a stronger influence than do others, of course. Among strong personalities, the wallflower in the group may be overlooked. Your influence may be overshadowed or unnoticed, but it will never be neutral.

Have you ever been selected to participate in a consumer survey or an opinion poll? If so, did you do it? It's possible that you were either too busy or too little interested to share your thoughts. Or perhaps you were miffed at the company, disgruntled about politics, or just didn't want to participate. But here's the thing: even by not responding, you were telling the pollster *something*. The motivation behind your message may have been unclear, but you did deliver a message. You said, "No."

When you come home and don't speak to your spouse, you're not being neutral. You're sending a negative message (or a positive one, if you're allowing them to focus on a task). When you don't raise your hand in class, you're sending a message—perhaps that you're bored, or don't understand, or are shy, or that the instructor hasn't reached you yet. It's impossible to be in any social context and exert no influence whatsoever. Your attitudes, words, and actions—or nonactions—say something.

That doesn't mean you always have to speak, always have to participate, or always have to respond. Of course not. But it does mean you must be aware that your influence—even through the nonverbal vibe you transmit to others—is never zero. It will always be either positive or negative.

Again, review your last 24 hours. Think about the times when you were the least available or the least open to others. What message did that send? Was it something positive, like, "I'm focused on being productive," or "I need sleep," or "Can we do this later?" Or was it a more negative message, like, "You're not important," or "I'm too busy for you," or "I don't want to deal with this"?

Remember that many aspects of your influence are subtle. They can be communicated even by facial expressions and nonverbal clues like a sigh, a groan, or a giggle. What did you communicate to others when you thought you were communicating nothing at all? By asking yourself that question, you are beginning to take control of your influence so you can leverage its possibilities.

Influence Is Variable

Dwelling on the power of your influence can seem a bit overwhelming. You may be thinking, *I can't do this! There's just so much to wrap my mind around.* It's not uncommon to feel a bit helpless and overwhelmed when contemplating a life change. You may feel it's impossible to develop the level of your influence for a variety of reasons.

One reason is that you may feel a lack of control over your life. Perhaps you have seen yourself as a passive person or you've been surrounded by dominant personalities. When others have exerted control over you, it can be difficult to think of yourself as having the power to change.

As a result, you may have fallen into a pattern of learned helplessness. You may have developed the lifestyle of allowing life to happen around you, passively accepting the outcome of situations or the decisions of others in a fatalistic way.

Third, you may have fallen for the idea that your life cannot be changed. "This is just who I am," you may say. "I'm a failure," or "I'm a weak-willed person," or "I'm a nobody." Your false belief system limits you to thinking that you must accept life as it now is, that no positive change is possible.

None of that is true. It is possible to change your life. You have the freedom to make choices for yourself. Your previous ways of looking at the world, seeing yourself, and interacting with others do not have to determine your future. You have the ability to control how you influence others. Your influence is variable.

If you have fallen into a pattern of thinking negatively and thus projecting a negative attitude to the world, that can change. *You* can change! If you have simply allowed life to happen, accepting whatever comes as if you have no choice, that can be changed too. You can exercise your freedom to make choices, form responses, build new relationships and sever old ones. If you have believed that you are the sum total of your past actions—especially your past mistakes and failures—that can change. Your past does not have to define you. You have the power to define yourself.

Think of the butterfly. These beautiful, delicate creatures are loved by nearly everyone for their colorful wings and airy flight. Of course, they begin life looking—and behaving—very different, as caterpillars. These wiggly worms have 13 body segments, and most are a dull brown color. They inch along the ground and crawl up plant stems, nibbling on organic matter. In order to grow larger, the caterpillar must molt, shedding its own skin four or five times before entering its cocoon. No one unfamiliar with the life cycle of the butterfly would think much of a caterpillar. These lethargic creatures don't show much potential.

Yet before the butterfly emerges from the cocoon, a great transformation has taken place. Fuzzy feelers have been replaced by graceful wings. The dull color has changed to bright orange, yellow, or purple hues. The drab insect that inched along the earth is now capable of gliding above it, some at speeds of up to 30 miles per hour!

Like the caterpillar, you can be transformed from dull to colorful, passive to active. Your influence over others may once have been slight, or it may have been largely negative in the past. No matter. You can influence yourself by changing your thoughts, and you can influence others to follow you through the positive power of your attitudes, words, and actions. Your influence need not remain what it is today. You have the power to change, and by changing, to change the world.

BE THE ONE

We are living at a time when the power of influence is clearly on display, a time when positive influence is sorely needed. Fake news, social media trolls, and widespread suspicion of others have combined to create a culture of outrage. It seems that each day brings louder shouting, less communicating, and a greater gap between well-meaning folks who happen to hold different opinions. We desperately need more people to realize the tremendous power of influence and to use it in positive ways.

This situation is not unlike one that occurred some 2,500 years ago in the ancient nation of Judah. This nation had wandered far from its roots and become riddled with corruption. God said in Ezekiel 22:29, "The people of the land practice extortion and commit robbery; they oppress the poor and needy and mistreat the foreigner," denying them justice. Verse 30 adds that God looked for someone who would rebuild the nation and "stand...in the gap on behalf of the land" in order to avoid its destruction.[4] But no one was found, and, sadly, the nation was destroyed.

We too are in need of leaders who will "stand in the gap" on behalf of their families, their communities, and even their country. The world seems filled with negative influences, those who degrade society through their negative attitude, careless words, and hostile actions. The stakes have never been higher, and people are desperately searching for positive influencers.

Will you be "that guy" or "that girl" who reverses the tide in your home, workplace, school, or community? Will you harness the subtle, dynamic, irresistible power of your attitude to create positive change? I think you are the one who can say to those around you, "We're better than this." When you lead through the power of your influence, others will follow. I believe in you.

THE KEY THREE

1. Did any section of this chapter cause you to reflect on your influence in a new light?

2. Be honest with yourself: Is your influence on others currently trending positive or negative?

3. What motivates you to be a positive influence on others?

THREE DIMENSIONS OF YOUR PERSONAL IMPACT

If you want to make an impact, start with yourself.

−JOHN C. MAXWELL[1]

A political election may be the ultimate test of influence. In countries from Andorra to Zimbabwe, Australia to Zambia, candidates periodically vie to be the people's choice for president, prime minister, or other offices at the head of state. It's no easy task to influence the thinking and decision-making of millions, sometimes hundreds of millions, of people.

In a recent presidential election in France, 11 candidates squared off in the first round, each hoping to gain the support of a majority of the country's millions of voters. As you can imagine, each politician faced a serious challenge in getting his or her message to the people. France is a nation of nearly 67 million people covering more than 248,000 square miles. The previous candidate to win a presidential election in France spent more than 20 million euros on the campaign. The barriers of time, travel, and communication are enormous in such an undertaking. How do you multiply your influence in order to reach millions of people in a short time? That's the question each candidate faced.

Jean-Luc Mélenchon, representing one of France's minority parties, knew that he would have to get creative in order to compete for votes. So the 65-year-old politician found a way to multiply his presence while conserving precious campaign funds. Mélenchon appeared live onstage at a rally in Lyon (eastern France), while a holographic image of himself was projected via satellite to crowds in six other cities, including one on the island of La Réunion, a French territory in the Indian Ocean, some 5,600 miles away![2] Critics called it a gimmick, but they simply may have been sorry they didn't think of it first.[3] Using technology, Mélenchon was able to appear live and in 3-D to supporters across the globe. He multiplied his influence—in three dimensions.

While Mélenchon's hologram may have been a new use of technology for swaying voters, three-dimensional influence is nothing new. In fact, to be effective, all influence must be cast in three dimensions: *self*, *others*, and *the world*. In this chapter, you will come to understand the three dimensions of influence and realize the vital importance of maintaining integrity in each one—especially the self.

INFLUENCE STEW

Influence exists in three dimensions, and they are always interrelated. The first dimension is *self*. To influence others, you must first influence yourself by taking control of your thoughts and attitudes. The second dimension of influence is *others*. This may be what you think of first when hearing the term *influence*. The third dimension of influence is *the world*, or people at a distance from you—those you don't personally interact with. These folks know you by your reputation, your work, or your communications. This widest dimension of influence is what Mélenchon exercised via hologram. He wanted to move the hearts and minds—not to mention the votes—of people who would never know him personally. To do so, he presented, well, himself.

That makes the point that these dimensions are not discrete or separate from one another. They are and must be interconnected. You cannot influence others to have a positive attitude if you do not have one yourself. Though that may sound obvious, it isn't always. And you cannot hope to influence the world if you do not first exert that same influence on those around you. There's no sense trying to persuade the people who don't know you to follow you, when the people who know you best will not. Like the hologram, which presents a whole person in three dimensions, all dimensions of your influence must be in sync, fully integrated with one another.

Another way to think of influence is as a stew. If you were to make a beef stew, for example, you'd probably want these three basic elements: meat, potatoes, and gravy. Those classic ingredients, seasoned with a few spices, would make a delicious meal. And you'd need all three. Meat and potatoes without the gravy wouldn't be a stew. Nor would gravy and meat alone. All three elements must be present to make the stew. But when you eat the stew, where does one ingredient end and another begin? You might take a bite that's mostly meat and another that's mostly potatoes, but the beauty of the stew is that all elements are more or less equally present. That's what gives it the flavor.

Your influence is the same way. It cannot exist without impacting all three dimensions—self, others, world—in similar ways. There's a word to describe those who attempt to exert influence while missing one of these key dimensions: *hypocrite.* If you fail to keep connected and consistent in each of the three dimensions, you will undermine your own influence and, quite possibly, harm your reputation. To be successful in influencing others, which is likely your primary goal, you must maintain the integrity of your influence.

Let's take a look at each of the three dimensions of influence. As we do, consider the ways you must grow in one dimension or another if you are to achieve your goals.

INFLUENCING YOURSELF

The first dimension in which you exercise influence may seem unlikely. We usually think of influence as something either that we exert over others or that others exert over us. Even the concept of influencing yourself may seem strange, as if you were two or more different people inhabiting the same life. But isn't that what you are?

Freudian psychologists speak of the id, the ego, and the superego as three aspects of the self. The id refers to our baser instincts; the superego to the moralizing, critical-thinking aspect of ourselves; and the ego to the executive function that mediates the two. Ancient religions sometimes refer to the three aspects of self as body, mind, and spirit. The apostle Paul also referred to a divide in the human nature, labeling one part the "old self" and the other the "new self." The first is riddled with selfish desires and prone to repeated failures, and the other is set free by faith in Christ and able to gain self-mastery.[4] Others have comically pictured these aspects of human nature as a devil sitting on one shoulder and an angel on the other, each whispering into our ear to influence us.

Whether or not you have thought of it in such terms before, you've certainly experienced this battle within yourself. One part of you wants to be disciplined, eat properly, and exercise regularly. The other part wants to eat junk food, sit on the couch, and relax. One part of you wants to save money, get out of debt, and live responsibly. The other part of you loves to spend money without counting the cost. No doubt you've won and lost countless such battles with yourself over the years. The term often used to describe this struggle to follow our better nature is *self-discipline*. However, I prefer the term *self-influence*.

Regardless of the terminology we place around this dynamic of self-influence, it is vital for success in every aspect of life, especially in influencing others. Self-influence is not simply a spiritual virtue or a psychological attribute with no bearing on "real life." It is a basic survival skill for beings, and it's the bedrock of influencing others. If you cannot influence yourself to be disciplined, kind, loving, or fair, you can never hope to cultivate that attribute in others. Your own failure in that area will be evident to all, undercutting your influence.

The old saying goes that you cannot take someone to a place you've never been, and, in terms of influence, that's true. You will never cultivate in others the character, mind-set, attitudes, and behaviors you do not display yourself. If you would influence others to follow you, you must first lead yourself. As has often been said, "You must be the change you want to see in the world."

How do you influence yourself? Obviously, this battle for self-mastery is a complicated challenge for human beings. It's written about in some of the most ancient spiritual writings, and it continues to be a subject of debate among psychologists. Many books have been written on the subject, and several of the chapters in this book deal with various aspects of self-mastery. For now, let's begin with the most basic step. To influence yourself, you must choose to take control of your own life.

Does that sound obvious? Believe me, it is not. Many people live with the mistaken idea that they are helpless. Realizing there are many things in life that they cannot control—such as the weather, the economy, the behavior of others, or the past—they conclude that they have no control over anything, including their own thoughts and actions. They become victims to the will of the id, the "old self," or the devil on their shoulder. They lack self-discipline and suffer the consequences of their inaction in the form of ill health, debt, or unhappiness.

If that describes you, I have good news. You *can* change. You may not have the power to change other people, and you certainly can't change the past, but you can change the future, beginning today. You can choose to think positive thoughts. You can choose to react positively in the face of adversity. You can choose to be active rather than passive. And all of that begins with your basic choice to take control of your own life—to influence yourself.

If you have not realized your need to influence yourself, make the choice to do it starting today. Resolve that you will not maintain a victim mind-set, passively accepting the version of yourself that you have created over the years—or that others have influenced you to be. Choose to become the person you hope to influence others to be.

Yes, this will take time. Self-influence is a lifelong endeavor. All the more reason to start today.

INFLUENCING OTHERS

The second dimension of influence is others, meaning the people with whom you are in direct contact. These are your family members, friends, classmates, coworkers, neighbors, or any person with whom you interact in the course of a day—even store clerks or passersby on the street. Remember, your influence is continual, and it is never neutral. Every day you exert influence on the people you see—or who see you. Following are a few things to keep in mind about your influence on others.

Your influence over others is important because it is the launch pad for your influence on the world. The people who know you the best should trust you the most, so if you cannot influence your loved ones, your friends, and others who have a direct window into your character, your influence will never grow wider. This concept has been a basic tenet of leadership theory for centuries and is even recorded in the Bible. The apostle Paul wrote to a young man named Timothy, giving him advice on appointing leaders in the fledgling churches of the first century. Paul wrote, "If anyone does not know how to manage his own family, how can he take care of God's church?"[5] If the people closest to you don't respect and trust you, it's likely that no one else will either.

This does not mean that every single person you meet must think highly of you if you are to extend your influence. Some of us are surrounded by irrational or dysfunctional people. And everyone has one or two people in their lives with whom they simply don't click. Even the greatest leaders are not able to influence everyone. However, if your good character is not evident to those close to you, generally resulting in trust and respect, your influence on the world will remain limited.

Also, the old adage holds true: you don't get a second chance to make a first impression. Internet entrepreneur and social media guru Gary Vaynerchuk is known for his animated style, and a quote often attributed to the energetic pitchman says, "I influence anybody who is able to get through the chaos of my first impression." Hopefully, lots of people push through that first impression to learn from the bestselling author of *The Thank You Economy*. However, you should not count on others being willing to battle through your bad attitude, complaining, anger, or negativity in order to get to know the "real you." From the looks and gestures you exchange with other drivers on the freeway to the casual words you say to store clerks, your first impression, like scent or shadow, precedes you wherever you go. Get it right, and it will open the door to positive influence. Blow that first impression, and you may permanently lose your opportunity to impact that person.

The tremendous potential of one person's influence over others was evident in the handling of an overbooked flight from Chicago's O'Hare Airport to Louisville, Kentucky. Airline personnel asked whether four passengers on Flight 3411 would be willing to step off the plane and take a later flight. Three people volunteered, but a fourth was involuntarily "bumped" from the flight. The man selected was a 69-year-old physician who not only refused to give up his seat, but also refused to cooperate with airport security personnel who were called to forcibly remove him. Cell phone cameras recorded the scene as the man was literally dragged kicking and screaming from the airplane. Within a short time, the videos were shared on social media and picked up by the mainstream press. The fallout was swift and substantial, as public opinion quickly swung against the airline for what seemed to be heavy-handed tactics. The airline's stock plummeted amid threats of a boycott, doing great damage to the carrier's reputation.[6] The lawsuit filed by the disgruntled passenger turned out to be the least of the airline's problems.

Though that situation was complex and I make no judgment about the persons directly involved, it's obvious that the airline's ability to attract other potential passengers and investors was harmed by a bad interaction with a single customer. The airline's influence on *others* (in this case, a particular person with whom they had direct contact) hampered their influence on *the world* (everyone else).

Carefully cultivate your influence over the people with whom you have contact each day. They are your gateway to reaching the world.

INFLUENCING THE WORLD

The third dimension of influence is the world: those who are at one remove from you. This includes the people you communicate with on social media but do not personally know; those who read your books or listen to your speeches; the people who buy your products or benefit from the money you donate to various causes. In the electronic age in which we live, this realm of influence could truly include the whole world. Your vision for change may be more modest than that, and you may be thinking primarily of influencing your community, or the people you work with, or perhaps just your family. That's fine. But remember that your influence *will* operate in this wider context whether you wish for it to or not. The world is socially connected, and not just through the Internet. Your reputation, your work, and your legacy may travel far beyond the people you influence day by day.

Your influence in this wider context can be summed up in a single word: *reputation.* Those who don't know you personally may still come to know *about* you. People who work at the same company you do will know whether or not you have a volatile temper long before they meet you face to face, if they ever do. Your selfless acts of kindness or sacrifice may become known to people you will never meet, influencing them to display the same virtues.

Your reputation has great power, partly because it is impersonal. Those who know you—your family and friends—will never believe all the best about you, nor all the worst. They know you well enough to realize that you are not a saint, but they still love you. They can overlook your faults and foibles. They can fill in the blanks with their personal knowledge of your character. Those at one remove, however, have nothing but your reputation to go by. They will fill in the rest with their imagination, for better or worse.

For that reason, you must guard your reputation carefully. It is one of your most precious—and most fragile—assets. Investor Warren Buffett, the Sage of Omaha, said, "It takes twenty years to build a reputation and five minutes to ruin it. If you think about that, you'll do things differently."[7]

Perhaps no one knows that better than Justine Sacco, the public relations executive who became an object of widespread criticism for a single careless remark made on social media. Before boarding a flight from London's Heathrow Airport to Cape Town, South Africa, Sacco tweeted this comment: "Going to Africa. Hope I don't get AIDS. Just kidding. I'm white!"

Justine Sacco had just 170 followers on Twitter. Her comment was likely meant as a jest to those closest to her, never intended for a wider audience. But during the 11-hour intercontinental flight, her tweet traveled also, making its way around the globe. Her comment went viral on social media, reaching far beyond her inner circle of friends and associates. Without intending to, Justine Sacco had influenced the world.

Sacco later said the statement was intended as an ironic comment on white privilege, but while she slept on the plane it was taken literally by thousands of social media users who were quick to voice their outrage. When Sacco turned on her phone upon landing in South Africa, it was flooded with messages. One person she knew from long ago acquaintance wrote, "I'm so sorry to see what's happening." Then another friend called to say, "You're the No. 1 worldwide trend on Twitter right now." Many angry readers had begun to castigate Sacco online and demand her firing, seeming to revel in her humiliation. Her parent company issued a statement saying, "This is an outrageous, offensive comment. Employee in question currently unreachable on an intl flight." Sacco later told a reporter how losing the respect of nearly everyone affected her. "I cried out my body weight in the first 24 hours," she said. "It was incredibly traumatic." And, as the faceless mob had demanded, she was fired from her job.[8]

Your influence over yourself, others, and the world are all connected. The words you say, even inside your own head or to your closest associates, can have a wider impact than you can imagine. As D.L. Moody reportedly once said, take care of your character, and your reputation will take care of itself. Maintain the integrity of your influence in all three dimensions.

INFLUENCE IN ACTION

The stories just mentioned show the tremendous danger in mismanaging your influence. Yet there is also tremendous potential to affect others for the good when your influence over yourself, others, and the world are in perfect alignment.

On June 12, 1929, a little girl was born to a Jewish couple, Otto and Edith, who were living in Germany. Fearing the coming persecution of Jews under the Nazi regime, Otto moved his family of four to the Netherlands in the late 1930s. But no place in Europe was safe from the Holocaust, and the family was forced into hiding. There, this child, now a girl of 13, spent the next 25 months hidden in the annex of rooms above Otto's office in Amsterdam, kept secret and aided by a few close friends of the family. The girl occupied her time by reading and by writing in her diary.

The girl wrote about all of the things you might expect an adolescent girl to be concerned with. She wrote about her family, the others who were also confined in the annex, and her hopes and dreams for the future. The remarkable thing, however, is how she, still a child, was able to maintain positive thoughts and a confident outlook in what must have been a frightful and depressing situation. Living in virtual captivity, she was able to influence herself to remain cheerful, positive, and hopeful about the future. That attitude had an impact on her family and others who knew her.

In time, however, the family was betrayed to the Nazis. They were arrested and deported to concentration camps. In March of 1945, nine months after her arrest, this young girl, now fifteen years old, died of typhus.

By now you may have guessed that this child was Anne Frank. Her diary, saved during the war by one of the family's helpers, was first published in 1947. Since then, *The Diary of a Young Girl* by Anne Frank has been translated into more than 60 languages.

It has sold more than 30 million copies, making it one of the bestselling books of all time and one of the most widely read books in the world.[9]

Because she was able to influence herself to be positive, kind to others, and hopeful, Anne Frank had tremendous influence over her family and their close friends. And because she was able to influence others, they preserved her words for publication, and Anne Frank has exerted tremendous influence on millions of people around the world.

Of all the words in Anne Frank's diary, perhaps the most moving are these, which should be a grand inspiration to every person who aspires to make a positive change: "I want to go on living even after my death! And therefore, I am grateful to God for giving me this gift, this possibility of developing myself and of writing, of expressing all that is in me."[10] She also said, "How lovely to think that no one need wait a moment, we can start now, start slowly changing the world!"[11] "We all know that 'example is better than precept.' So set a good example, and it won't take long for others to follow."[12]

This is the power of influence in three dimensions. When you influence yourself, you influence others. When you influence others, you reach the world. So what are you waiting for?

THE KEY THREE

1. How would you describe the connection between the three levels of influence?

2. In what ways do you need to influence yourself more positively?

3. Who are the people you influence on a daily basis, and what is the result of that influence?

Part 2

CULTIVATING YOUR PERSONAL IMPACT

THE POWER OF YOUR VISION

*All our dreams can come true if we have
the courage to pursue them.*

WALT DISNEY[1]

If you had been traveling by train from the town of Banbury, England, to London on the morning of April 6, 2015, you'd have been in for a surprise. Passengers on the First Great Western service from that market town along the Oxford Canal had settled in for the 64-mile jaunt to London when crewmembers hopped aboard and put the commuter train in motion. Only instead of heading east, toward London, they drove the train west, toward Swansea. The direction was not a mistake; the crew meant to go to Swansea. That was their assignment. The problem was that they had boarded the wrong train. They had a destination in mind, but they were still headed in the wrong direction.

The crew soon realized their mistake and headed back to Banbury station. Passengers had to catch the next train, causing them to arrive late at their destination. "We are really sorry," said a company spokesman. "Unfortunately the train crew boarded the wrong train."

One person tweeted, "I'd have thought this was page 1 of the Train Driver's Manual." He added good-naturedly, "But then I've made pretty stupid mistakes at work too."[2]

In fact, nearly everyone has made that identical error—setting out in the wrong direction and taking others along for the ride. That's precisely what happens when we exercise influence without vision. We don't know where we're going, and we lead others on the same chase.

Possibly you've been on both sides of this situation, as a driver and a passenger. Perhaps when you were younger, you idolized a friend who you thought was cool. Maybe you adopted their manner of speech and copied their attitudes, only to find that their personality or outlook completely changed within a few months. Though you thought they had it all together, they were really just finding themselves. That's influence without vision.

Or you may have worked for a company that announced a grand, new corporate strategy, only to abandon it within a few weeks. It became clear that the leaders had no firm direction. They exercised influence without vision.

You may have done this yourself, strongly voicing an opinion and urging others to adopt your point of view, only to change your mind. You were able to influence others but did not have a clear vision of the future you wanted to create.

Influence without vision is, at best, a waste of time. At worst, it's a danger to you and your community because it erodes trust, squanders resources, and could lead others to a place they have no desire to be. If it is true that you can't take others to a place you've never been, it's also true that you can't take others to a destination when you don't know where it is. If you hope to have lasting influence, you must have a clear vision.

What happens when you have both vision and influence? Well, just about anything. It is a powerful combination that leads to real change in people's lives and in the world.

A strong, positive vision both guides your life choices and serves as an inviting call to others, attracting them to join you. In this chapter, you will learn how to form, articulate, and communicate the change you hope to make in the world, thus influencing others to join you.

WHAT VISION IS

First, let's define what vision is. Vision is your preferred version of the future, the positive change you are trying to make in yourself and others. Simply put, your vision is the change you want to see in the world. You've probably seen before-and-after pictures, the photos people take before and after they begin their diet or undertake some renovation project. Laid side by side, these photos make a dramatic illustration of the change that has occurred, whether it's weight loss, home improvement, or new construction. The contrast is often inspiring.

The problem, of course, is that you don't have before-and-after pictures of yourself or your house before you begin the project. All you can see is the now—the problem that exists. You see the weight you want to lose. You see the outdated kitchen appliances or the vacant space.

To get yourself motivated on your own project, you must *envision* a future reality that doesn't yet exist. What we call vision is the "after" photo that exists only in your mind. It's a picture of the reality you're trying to create. To make any worthwhile change in your life, your community, or your world, you must be able to see that preferred future. You must have a mental image of the change you want to make in the world.

Lack of vision is the reason most well-intentioned leaders are not able to produce the change they long for. They may understand that the world is not right, or that something in their personal life, family, or workplace isn't functioning as it should be. But it takes no vision to name the problem. Everyone can see it! It requires no foresight to realize that you are in poor physical condition, or your company is losing money, or the streets in your town are riddled with potholes. Problems are always obvious. What's not so clear is the compelling idea of what *could* be if people are willing to work for change. Stating the problem requires nothing more than good eyesight. To see the future, well, that takes vision.

Let's pause right here and return to the central question of this book: What is the change you hope to make in the world? You may be thinking primarily of the problem and stating your "vision" in those terms. For example, you may say, "I'm overweight," or "I wish I wasn't in debt," or "Our company keeps losing money." Each statement certainly represents a problem in need of a solution, but that is not a vision. A vision is a clear, compelling view of the *future,* not the problems of the present. Examine these statements and see if you notice the difference from the ones above:

- I see myself fit, healthy, and having energy to do the things that matter to me.

- My family is debt free and gives generously to worthy causes.

- My company is thriving and has the capital to enter new markets.

Do you notice the difference? Problem statements are flat and uninspiring. They are often demotivating because they focus attention on what's wrong. While it's vital to face the reality of your situation squarely, no matter how bleak it may seem, you cannot hope to produce change by dwelling on the problems of the present. You must look to the future and see an inspiring, positive, hopeful image of what *will* be. And that brings us to the real value of vision, how it functions in your life and how it translates into influence in the lives of others.

HOW VISION WORKS

The first function of a strong vision is that it becomes your guide into the future, telling you which direction to take. If you have a clear vision, you'll drive your train in the right direction every time. If you have a smartphone or a GPS, you already know the value of this kind of navigation system. A GPS uses triangulation to tell you two vital pieces of information: where you are and the location of your destination. A global positioning system can calculate your location on the planet within a few feet by measuring the time it takes a signal to travel between a system of satellites and a receiver—the handheld unit you refer to as a GPS.[3] It tells you where you are. In vision terms, that's like stating the problem. But the GPS can tell you something more: the location of your destination. When you know those two things— where you are and where you want to be—you always know which direction to take.

That's the first function of vision in your life. You already know where you are (that is, the problems you face), but vision tells you where you want to be. By comparing the two, you will always have a foolproof guide for making decisions about what to do next. You know which way to travel because you can clearly see where you want to wind up.

Let's translate that into real-world terms using a couple of the examples we've already mentioned. If your vision is to be fit, healthy, and energetic, then you will have clarity about what to do when offered the opportunity to skip your bike ride or have a second slice of pizza for lunch. The answer to both is no. Why? Because you can see your destination, and you know that both of those options are detours away from it.

If your vision is to be debt free, then the questions "Should we buy a new computer on credit?" and "Will we pay more than the minimum on our credit card payment?" both have obvious answers. No, you won't take on further debt, and yes, you will sacrifice to make progress on repayment. The first is a detour away from your destination; the second is a giant step toward it.

That's the power of vision. It gives you a clear picture of where you are in relation to where you want to be. It guides your path into the future.

A second function of vision relates not to you but to others. Just as vision is a GPS to guide your decision making, it is also a beacon, guiding others toward a future they may not have been able to see for themselves.

For centuries, beacons of various types have guided voyagers to their destinations. Signal fires, lighthouses, and, now, electronic signals have given ship captains and pilots a clear indication of the path toward a port, around a shoal, or onto a runway. A beacon tells others, "This way!" And that's precisely what your vision will do for those around you. It will guide them toward a destination they can't clearly see on their own.

Many people long for this sense of direction in their lives but have difficulty articulating a vision for change. Yet when a leader comes along and says, "Here's what's possible for our family" (or company or community or church), others latch on to that signal like a fighter jet locked on to the approach beacon of an aircraft carrier. Though they may not be able to define the vision themselves, they will recognize it when they see it and will be readily influenced by it.

When Dr. Martin Luther King Jr. spoke of a world in which people would "not be judged by the color of their skin but by the content of their character," he articulated a vision that few would have imagined, but multitudes latched onto it.[4] That speech, in part, led to profound changes in American society.

When President John Kennedy stood in front of a joint session of Congress and announced, "I believe that this nation should commit itself to achieving the goal, before this decade is out, of landing a man on the moon and returning him safely to the earth," he excited the imagination of a nation that had never dreamed of such a venture.[5] Yet that bold vision became a shining beacon for a generation, inspiring the nation to meet that goal in just eight years.

This is the power of vision in action. A strong, positive vision acts as a beacon for others, rousing them from apathy, lethargy, and exhaustion, and motivating them to create change.

When you form your vision and begin to share it, your ideas will become a guiding light for others to follow. Your family members, neighbors, and fellow students will be rallied to the dream of a changed world. Who knows? You might even inspire a nation.

VISION INHIBITORS

If vision is such a natural way to motivate oneself and influence others, why don't more people have a clear, compelling vision of the future? Like most things, creating and sharing a positive vision is easier said than done. The reason is that there are powerful forces at work against anyone who dares to dream and to inspire others with that dream. As a would-be influencer, you must be aware of the factors that inhibit your ability to create and cast a vision. Following are three powerful vision killers. Two of them reside within you, and the third you will encounter in others.

Fear

Whether we like admitting it or not, most of us are afraid of change. All change, even positive change, brings with it the unknown. The moment you begin to dream of a different reality, you will be confronted with questions about the future. You intuitively realize that creating change in any context will alter the status quo of relationships, economics, and other systems in your life. Though you may never voice these questions aloud, you will begin to wonder about things like these:

- How will standing up for my rights affect my relationships with my siblings?
- If I adopt a healthier lifestyle and my spouse doesn't, how will that affect our marriage?
- Will I lose friends if I change my habits of spending and socializing?
- Will I lose my job if I begin to push for changes at work?

Fear is a natural first reaction to the thought of change. Fear is a vision killer and, therefore, an influence killer. To influence others in a positive direction, you must first face and conquer the fears that reside within you. Vision requires courage.

Are you willing to work for change in your life and in your relationships, even though there are risks involved? Are you more committed to your vision for the future than to the status quo? Have you counted the cost of making changes in your world? You must risk in order to grow.

Self-Doubt

The second barrier to vision is *self-doubt*. Dreaming about the future is much easier when you're alone at home, envisioning the world as you'd like it to be. Yet as soon as you step outside your door, you're forced to face this simple reality: you are just one person, and the world is an awfully big place. You become keenly aware of your own shortcomings, and you begin to ask questions like these:

- Can I really make my vision reality?
- Was I foolish for thinking things can really change?
- What if I fail?
- Who am I to take on this challenge?

- What if nobody listens to me?
- Am I smart enough, strong enough, or good enough to make this happen?

Self-doubt is the devil on your shoulder, continually whispering into your ear, "You must have been crazy to think this was possible!" Self-doubt is a perfectly normal experience, and, sadly, it stops many would-be influencers in their tracks. Paralyzed by these inner demons, they quietly decide that it's simpler and safer to put their vision on the shelf and accept things the way they are.

To form and share your vision with others, you will need self-confidence. This is not an inflated sense of self that leads you to believe you have no weaknesses and can do things that are beyond your ability. Self-confidence is a proper sense of your own worth that leads you to believe that if others can succeed, you can too. You do have what it takes to be a dreamer, a doer, an influencer. Are you ready to stop listening to the voice of doubt and doom and tune in to the voice of faith, hope, and possibility? Are you willing to believe that you—yes, *you*—can make a positive change in the world? If so, you're ready to influence others.

Resistance

The third force that works against vision is not internal but external. It is the *resistance* you will meet in others when you begin to exercise influence. All change is initially met with this resistance because all people feel the same feelings of fear and self-doubt when the possibility of change is presented. Every person you meet will be wondering about the same questions that you have faced. However, unlike you, they will have an object for their negative emotions—you. As the one presenting a vision for change, you will become the focus of their negative energy. This resistance may take shape in passivity, hostility, avoidance, undermining, or outright conflict. When that happens, just remember you also had to work through your fears and doubts about this vision. Allow others the opportunity to do that as well, but don't allow their resistance to inhibit your dreams, or the sharing of those dreams with others.

Are you willing to face the pushback of family members, friends, and even total strangers concerning your vision? Then you are ready to become an influencer.

KEEPING IT SIMPLE

As you form your ideal for a positive future, be careful to articulate that vision in terms that will inspire both you and others. A common mistake among those who seek change is that their vision for the future is too complex to be easily understood. To be influential, your vision must be simple, inspiring, and easy to remember. But you would be surprised at how complex some vision or mission statements are.

Now consider this statement from the Alzheimer's Association: "Our vision: A world without Alzheimer's disease."[6] Or this from Oxfam: "Our vision is a just world without poverty."[7] It's likely that either of those statements could inspire your interest in joining the cause, or at least learning more about it. The most influential statements of vision are clear, concise, specific, and inspiring.

What do you hope to achieve? How do you want to influence others? Consider these statements that articulate some common personal dreams.

- My vision is to lose 30 pounds in one year.
- I will be debt free in two years.
- My dream is a 100 percent graduation rate.
- We can end discrimination in our workplace.

If you cannot state your dream for the future in a single sentence, it may not be clear to others—or even to you. If it takes more than five to ten words, it probably won't be inspiring. But when you can see it clearly, state it briefly, and repeat it easily to others, your positive picture of the future will influence many to join you.

FROM VISION TO INFLUENCE

Having a positive, inspiring vision for the future is a first step to influencing others. But that vision will have little effect it if is printed on a business card and tucked into a drawer, or posted on a web page that nobody visits. To affect others with your vision, that vision must exert a positive force in your life and in theirs. There are two primary ways that takes place.

Live It

The first way to influence others with your vision is to *live it*. Your vision must be more than a slogan you repeat from time to time. It must actually influence *you* in the plans you choose, the decisions you make, and the way you live your life. John C. Maxwell said, "Good leaders must communicate vision clearly, creatively, and continually. However, the vision doesn't come alive until the leader models it."[8] Andy Stanley has coined the phrase "wear it" to describe this aspect of leadership. When it comes to creating change in an organization, Stanley says, "It's not enough to believe it. You must be seen doing it."[9]

To be credible in influencing others, you must be committed to enacting the changes you ask them to adopt. If you want others to be more respectful of each other in your home, then you must keep your temper in check and speak with kindness. If you hope to create a workplace in which each person is treated fairly, you must be generous in giving credit to others for their contributions and make room at the table for newcomers. You cannot hope to inspire others to create a world that you are not willing to sacrifice for yourself.

Repeat It

The second way to influence others with your vision is to *repeat it*. The Rule of Seven is an old marketing principle that holds that a prospect must see or hear a marketing message at least seven times before they will take action on it. That's why, for example, advertisers are willing to place their ads on television, radio, or websites until people are nearly sick of seeing them. The technical term for this is *effective frequency*. This has to do with the number of exposures that are necessary for a person to respond to an advertised message. Beyond that point, the exposure can become wasteful.

So what is the effective frequency of a vision? How many times does a person have to hear that positive idea of the future before they adopt it for themselves? How many times can you repeat your vision to others before they no longer care to hear it?

Many leadership experts would say that there is no effective frequency for vision. In other words, people must hear it constantly in order for it to become part of their thinking. And it is impossible to repeat a vision too often because people easily forget it or become distracted from pursuing it. In practical terms, this means that you must repeat your vision to others as often as you possibly can so that it becomes a natural part of their thinking and doesn't get crowded out by the busyness of life.

What does that look like? It's saying things like, "Remember, we're going to be debt free in two years" every time you make a decision about spending. It's saying to a coworker, "Good job with that project. We're well on our way to being the most innovative company in our industry." It means looking in the mirror every day and repeating the words, "I will be at my goal weight by my birthday," then saying it to your spouse each time you choose a restaurant. To influence others with your vision, it must become part of your vocabulary—and theirs.

When you are tired of talking about the positive change you hope to see in the world, you're just getting started with being an influencer. And when you begin to hear your vision repeated back to you by family members, coworkers, neighbors, and friends, you know that your influence is taking hold. Model your vision with every choice you make, and repeat it to others at every opportunity. As you do so, your influence will begin to grow.

THE RIGHT TRAIN

Let's return to the train platform in Banbury for a moment. Imagine yourself as a London-bound traveler who was inadvertently hijacked toward Swansea by a conductor who'd boarded the wrong train. You rode along for miles, knowing that you were bound for the wrong destination but unable to do anything about it. How do you suppose that would feel? What emotions would you experience? Frustration? Anger? Helplessness? Resignation? Now imagine your relief the moment the crew realized their error and stopped the train. They were still a long way from Banbury, and an even farther distance from London. But a critical change had been made. Someone had come to see that the train was headed in the wrong direction and had begun to do something about it.

Now that you have a clear vision for the future, you're like the train conductor who has realized the problem and begun to address it. You can't change your destination overnight, but you have already changed your direction. By adopting a positive vision for the future, you have taken the first critical step to changing your world. Even if your destination is still a thousand miles away, it feels much more empowering and hopeful to take one step toward it than to be sitting still or moving the other way.

You're on the right train now. You see a clear picture of a better future for yourself or your family or your workplace or the world. Now that vision can serve as your GPS, guiding your decisions from day to day. And the more often you enact that vision and repeat it to others, the more it will become their beacon, drawing them along with you. You have a clear picture of a preferred future, and that is the first step toward influencing others to follow. Your train is now headed in the right direction, and you are well on your way to changing the world.

· · · · · · · · · · · · · · · ·   **THE KEY THREE**   · · · · · · · · · · · · · · · ·

1. State your vision for the future in one sentence.

2. Name one life change you can make right now to act on that vision.

3. Tell one person about your vision and ask them to join you in making it reality.

THE POWER OF YOUR THOUGHTS

For as he thinketh in his heart, so is he.

PROVERBS 23:7 (KJV)

The train had just pulled out of Circular Quay Railway Station in Sydney for a ten-minute run to Central Station, the busiest rail port in New South Wales, Australia, serving some 11 million riders per year. Passengers sat quietly, as commuters often do, some reading and others looking out the window, possibly anxious about whatever events the day might bring.

Just then a railway employee came on the public-address system to make an announcement. Generally, live announcements—as opposed to prerecorded messages—are muffled and difficult to understand. Passengers often tune them out entirely, preferring to focus on their newsfeeds or listening to music through headphones. But on this day, ears perked up all over the train. Passengers who'd had their eyes glued to smartphones or tablets became attentive, listening to the conductor's message.

"Good morning, ladies, gentlemen, and children," the conductor said clearly and cheerfully. "This is the 7:35 a.m. from Penrith to Central, and you'll be pleased to know that we are right on time."

Smiles began to appear on the passengers' faces.

"This means that we'll get you to where you're going in plenty of time," the announcer continued, his voice animated, "and what a lovely morning it is in Sydney today. The sun is shining, temperature is about

21 degrees, birds are singing, and all's right with the world. I trust you have a great day wherever you're going. Thanks for catching my train this morning, and I hope to see you again soon."

The good mood proved to be contagious. By the time the announcement concluded, passengers were not only smiling but had even started connecting with one another. Perfect strangers struck up spontaneous conversations, something almost unheard of on a busy commuter train. Why? Because the cheerful attitude of the friendly conductor had done what a positive attitude will do anywhere in the world, in any context, with any group—it had influenced people to follow.[1]

You have probably experienced something like that before. When a coworker arrives showing visible enthusiasm for the day ahead, the whole team becomes energized. One person's positive attitude can influence an entire workplace. That can be true in a negative sense as well. When a flight is delayed, all it takes is one passenger to begin complaining, and a sour mood will infect the entire cabin.

Attitude is contagious. Like a yawn, it will spread from person to person, affecting the atmosphere of a family, classroom, office, or any other group. Your attitude, for better or worse, will influence those around you.

And here's something you may not know: you have the power to control your attitude through the thoughts you choose to entertain. How you think determines how you feel. How you feel shapes how you act and react in any situation. And your attitude—that is, your thoughts and feelings displayed through behavior—will influence any group you are in. All of that begins with the mind.

If you want to have a positive influence on others, you must have a positive outlook fueled by positive thoughts. If you allow yourself to engage in a negative thought pattern, that will work its way out into your words and actions, even your facial expressions. And that will negatively influence those around you. The ancient wisdom of the Bible rings true: "As [a man] thinks in his heart, so is he" (Proverbs 23:7 NKJV). Your thoughts determine your influence because they affect everything else about you.

In this chapter, you will come to understand why it is so important to take control of your thoughts, fueling your mind with a positive outlook. You'll also learn the seven types of positive thinking that will produce a positive influence. And what's more, you'll discover that, regardless of how negative you may have been in the past, you *can* change your mind and become a positive person. You can influence those around you with joy and hope. It all starts when you take control of your most valuable asset, your mind.

HOW POSITIVE THINKING CHANGES YOU

For centuries medical professionals have studied the human condition through the lens of disease. That means they have generally paid less attention to healthy people than to the sick, and they have focused their attention on what's wrong with an eye toward making it better. In other words, they've focused on the symptoms and root causes of illness and tried to alleviate or eliminate them. That has also been true in the relatively new medical specialty of psychology. It has been driven largely by the attempt to identify and eliminate mental illness.

However, there is an emerging focus on wellness in the practice of medicine, and that exists within the practice of psychology as well. *Positive psychology* focuses on fostering positive attitudes toward one's experiences, individual traits, and life events with the goal of minimizing destructive thoughts and creating a sense of optimism toward life. Positive psychology examines how ordinary people can become happier and more fulfilled.

Barbara L. Fredrickson, a researcher at the University of Michigan, found that positive thinking is more than just a feel-good exercise; it actually changes the way your brain works. In her experiment, Fredrickson divided her subjects into five groups and showed each group different video clips, each intended to foster a different kind of emotional response. The first group saw clips intended to create feelings of joy; the second, hope; the fourth, fear; and the fifth, anger. The third group was the control group, so they watched videos that were not intended to evoke any emotional response.

Afterward, Fredrickson asked each person to imagine themselves in a situation where they would experience similar emotions to what they'd just seen, and write down what they would do in response. Each person had a piece of paper with 20 blank lines that began with the words, "I would like to..."

Here's where it gets interesting. People who saw images that evoked fear or anger wrote down the fewest responses, but those who saw images of joy and contentment recorded many more. Fredrickson concluded that when we experience positive emotions like love, joy, and contentment, we see more possibilities for our lives. Positive emotions actually make you think bigger, while negative emotions limit your sense of possibility. Frederickson proposed that

> positive emotions *broaden* an individual's momentary thought-action repertoire: joy sparks the urge to play, interest sparks the urge to explore, contentment sparks the urge to savour and integrate, and love sparks a recurring cycle of each of these urges within safe, close relationships. The broadened mindsets arising from these positive emotions are contrasted to the narrowed mindsets sparked by many negative emotions (i.e., specific action tendencies, such as attack or flee).[2]

This means that when you dwell on negative thoughts such as complaining, worry, anger, anxiety, and unforgiveness, it shuts down your brain's ability to cope with problems and find solutions. But when you entertain thoughts of hope, love, and joy, you increase your mind's ability to solve problems and create a better future. Positive thinking actually changes your brain.

There's more. Fredrickson also proposed, "Positive emotions promote discovery of novel and creative actions, ideas and social bonds, which in turn *build* that individual's personal resources...These resources function as reserves that can be drawn on later to improve the odds of successful coping and survival."[3] Positive thoughts lead to increased "social bonds," which become a resource for the future. That's a complex way of saying that positive thinking increases your influence with others.

Fredrickson summarized her findings this way:

When positive emotions are in short supply, people get stuck. They lose their degrees of behavioural freedom and become painfully predictable. But when positive emotions are in ample supply, people take off. They become generative, creative, resilient, ripe with possibility and beautifully complex. The broaden-and-build theory conveys how positive emotions move people forward and lift them to the higher ground of optimal well-being.[4]

While it may have taken a psychological study for many to accept these ideas, they have been obvious to positive thinkers for centuries. Positive thinking results in a greater sense of personal well-being—plus, it increases your ability to solve problems, make friends, and influence others. The key to broadening your influence is something you already have: your mind. All you have to do is activate it with positive thoughts.

HOW YOUR THOUGHTS AFFECT YOUR INFLUENCE

The link between your thoughts and your influence is clear, and it's confirmed by the teaching of the Bible: "A good man brings good things out of the good stored up in his heart, and an evil man brings evil things out of the evil stored up in his heart. For the mouth speaks what the heart is full of."[5] What you harbor in your heart (or mind) eventually finds its way out into your words and actions. The face you present to the world—literally, the expression on your face—is a reflection of the thoughts within you. So it's not at all surprising that positive thoughts produce positive influence and vice versa. Let's explore that concept a bit, beginning with the effect of negative thinking.

Negative thinking adversely affects your influence in a number of ways. First, your negative thoughts become a *self-fulfilling prophecy.* That simply means that when you think negative thoughts about yourself or your situation, they are likely to come true. When you think you will fail, you are more likely to fail. When you think people won't like you, chances are good that they won't. Why? Because your negative thoughts begin to work themselves out in negative actions. You think you'll fail, so you don't prepare as well. What's the point? You become more nervous because you're expecting to bomb. You're worried about meeting others, so your hands become sweaty and you say very little. You have a worried look on your face. Those factors add up to reduced likeability. Your negative thoughts become a predictor of your negative influence.

Second, negative thinking *turns off others*. The problem with negative thinking is that it won't stay inside your head. It comes out through your teeth in the form of complaints, gossip, sighing, or fault finding. People are seldom willing to follow a naysayer.

Third, negative thinking *limits vision*. As Frederickson's research shows, when you dwell on fear, anger, and other negative feelings, your brain is not as well able to envision possibilities. You can't see what's possible; therefore, you're unable to share a positive vision with others. You don't become an influencer because you have no fresh alternatives to offer.

Finally, negative thinking results in *discouragement*. Negative thinkers ultimately become stuck where they are, unable to see a better future or move toward it. Their dour attitude is unattractive to others, so they lose whatever influence they may have had.

The good news, of course, is that positive thinking expands influence in the opposite direction. When you are a positive thinker, your positive thoughts become self-fulfilling prophecies that work in your favor. While that doesn't guarantee success, it improves the odds that you will influence others. When you have a positive attitude, you produce positive speech, demeanor, and facial expressions. You become the bright light in the room that everyone is drawn to, giving you an opportunity to influence them with your ideas. And you see possibilities. Positive thinking is like a shot of adrenaline for the brain, kicking it into high gear. It enables you to envision a better future—which is precisely the point at which you can influence others.

If you want to expand your influence, expand your mind. Fuel it with positive thoughts. Doing so will literally change your brain, making you better able to envision the future and enlist others to help you in creating it. How do you do that? Let's examine the kinds of positive thoughts that increase your influence over others.

SEVEN TYPES OF POSITIVE THINKING

We generally lump all types of positive thought under that one umbrella term—*positive thinking.* By doing so, we reduce a highly complex way of looking at the world to a simplistic metaphor: seeing the glass as either half-empty or half-full. Though *possibility thinking* is important—and we'll talk more about it shortly—positive thought includes much more than your first response to a situation. It is an outlook that affects virtually every aspect of your inner life. Following are seven types of positive thinking that will produce a dramatic change in your attitude and actions. Let's examine each one in order to understand the way it increases your influence over others.

1. Optimism

Optimism is often used as a catchall term for positive thinking, but let's explore what the word really means. The term can be traced to the philosopher Gottfried Wilhelm Leibniz, who concluded that the world in which we live is the "best (optimum) among all possible worlds."[6] In the best possible world, the best possible circumstances must exist and everything must be getting better rather than worse. So, classic optimism is usually seen as a naïve, unrealistic notion about the goodness of the world and the virtuous nature of human beings. But this is not at all what we mean by optimism as a form of positive thinking.

Of course, we know that evil exists in the world, so optimism is not a simplistic belief that all of life's circumstances are somehow good. Neither does optimism require a belief that the world is always getting better. We know from history that great evils have taken place again and again in the form of war, disease, and natural disaster. What we mean by optimism is the hopeful thought that better possibilities do exist and that they are in fact *more likely* to occur than negative ones. The optimist believes that, all things being equal, it'll probably all work out for the best. And usually it does.

For example, when the stock market takes a downturn, as it often does, one risk is that it will lead to a great crash, producing a worldwide economic depression in which millions are unemployed and people are left homeless and begging for food. That could happen. But an optimist knows that it probably won't, and doesn't spend time worrying about it. She believes that, while things may be more difficult for a time, she probably won't lose her job or house, and things will work out fine in the end. An optimist knows that when he is delayed by an accident on the freeway, it's possible that he'll miss the sales opportunity—but that's unlikely. More likely is that the client will understand that traffic can be unpredictable and will offer another chance to make the pitch.

Optimists think about what's most likely to happen rather than focusing on the less likely—and more frightful—things that probably won't come to pass. Therefore, optimists seldom waste brainpower on anxiety, worry, or gloomy thoughts about the future. That frees their minds to engage in creative possibilities and problem solving.

Optimists are more likely to influence others because optimism is a form of thought leadership. People are naturally drawn to positive thoughts and wish to avoid negative ones—even if they may be thinking them. As you give voice to the real probability that there are better days ahead, despite the current circumstances, others will listen to you. Remember, optimism does not mean dismissing problems or being unwilling to face challenges squarely. This is not a form of denial. It's a determination to focus on the best possible outcomes, then work to make them reality.

If you want to influence others, practice optimistic thinking. Don't allow your mind to dwell on frightening but remote possibilities. Spend your brainpower on the more likely, more positive outcomes of a situation. That positive thinking will draw others to you.

2. Humility

Humility may seem like an unlikely aspect of positive thinking, but the most positive thinkers are truly humble. What I mean by that is that they have a correct view of themselves. They see themselves accurately, neither thinking too much nor too little of their own worth and ability. That accurate understanding of themselves produces a high level of self-acceptance, which is an attractive character trait.

Interestingly, a very important aspect of positive thinking is to avoid thinking too highly of yourself. In the field of psychology, it has long been observed that most people tend to overestimate their own ability and undervalue the contributions of others. This bias was first noted by researchers David Dunning and Justin Kruger and is known as the Dunning-Kruger Effect. The pair found this odd phenomenon in their research. People who are not good at a certain task—like singing, for example—tend to overestimate their ability. In other words, they think they can sing really well when they can't. You've probably stood in church next to someone with a Dunning-Kruger bias. They belt out every song as if they were a great talent when they can barely carry a tune. The corollary to this effect is that people who have a high level of ability often underestimate themselves, thinking they're less talented than they really are.[7] You've probably encountered people like that too. Though they may be the most talented member of your team, they are reluctant to volunteer, saying, "Someone else can probably do it better." They're not kidding; they really believe that.

Another interesting phenomenon is that we often attribute our own success to internal factors—such as our intelligence, ability, charm, or personality—and attribute our failures to external factors: luck, the weather, or the misdealing of others. So when we succeed, it's because we're great, and when we fail, it's because we're unlucky. However, we're likely to reverse those categories for others. When they succeed, it's because of luck, and when they fail, it's because they're somehow inferior.

Humility is the antidote to this. Simply put, humility is the ability to see yourself accurately, neither inflating your own ability nor under-valuing your contribution—and seeing others in that same, honest way. Both errors (inflating a sense of ability or undervaluing contributions) often stem from an inadequate level of self-esteem. Those who inflate their ability and look askance at others often fear being seen as inferior to others. And those who undervalue themselves often fear rejection. The humble person has a proper sense of self-esteem, and therefore does not look to others for a sense of well-being. He or she can honestly say, "You know, I'm just not a good singer and I'm not afraid to admit that; maybe someone else should sing the solo," or "Yes,

I really am best qualified for this task, so I'll take it on." Humility is not thinking poorly of yourself, but seeing yourself honestly and accurately. And that's a very positive attitude.

Humble people are influential because their ego needs are very low. They are unjealous of the abilities and successes of others; they're never looking for "ego strokes" for the contributions they make; and they are not afraid to give praise or thanks to others. As a result, they are seen as trustworthy.

To grow in humility, spend some time examining yourself. Candidly appraise your strengths and weaknesses. Don't be afraid of this exercise. Welcome the opportunity to know yourself better. Accept who you are. Determine how you will change and grow. When you have done so, you will actually feel more positive about yourself and be less dependent on the need for external praise.

3. Abundance

When you have a good idea at work, do you tend to keep it quiet until you can act on it, thereby reserving the credit for yourself? Or do you share the idea with others at the first opportunity? When your coworker forgets her lunch, do you make a mental note to eat at your desk because you've only brought one sandwich? Or do you volunteer to share with her, knowing that the meal was barely enough to feed one, let alone two?

These real-world choices illustrate the difference between a *scarcity mind-set* and *abundance thinking*. The first set of reactions in each example illustrate a scarcity mind-set. This thinking is based on the idea that there is a limited amount of good in the world, barely enough to go around. It results in a desire to hoard everything from food to money to good ideas, keeping them to yourself in an effort to ensure that you have what you need. Scarcity thinking produces anxiety and worry about the future.

Abundance thinking is based on the opposite notion: seeing good as an infinite supply, something we can create at will. Abundance thinkers believe that "there's always more where that came from." As a result, they're willing to give away good ideas, share food, loan money (or give it away), and welcome others. They believe they'll have another good idea tomorrow, and that someone else will share with them when they are in need.

Though this may sound like folly, it's actually taught in the Bible. Jesus said, "Give, and it will be given to you. A good measure, pressed down, shaken together and running over, will be poured into your lap. For with the measure you use, it will be measured to you."[8] Abundance thinkers have found that this dictum is generally true. Sure, you'll meet stingy people once in a while. But when you share with others, they generally share with you too. Abundance thinking is not mere wishful thinking. It's built into the fabric of the universe.

Abundance thinkers are able to multiply their influence over others for several reasons. They are generous with others, and generosity is always rewarded. They are not threatened by apparent shortages of resources, and their worry-free minds are better able to find solutions. They are willing to include others who bring an unequal supply of resources or ability.

If you tend to see things from a scarcity point of view, it will at first be challenging to adopt an abundance mentality. When you feel yourself slipping into stinginess and hoarding, practice saying to yourself, "There's always more where that came from." You'll be amazed at how consistently that turns out to be true.

4. Openness

Positive thinkers are open-minded. That does not mean, as is sometimes thought, that they are willing to accept every new idea or that they have no firm convictions. Open-minded people do indeed hold firm ideas, but they are willing to change those ideas based on new information. Closed-minded people feel threatened by new information because they fear change. They have determined that they know all there is to know about business, parenting, marriage, politics, and life in general. Their worldview is a closed system, impenetrable even by facts and logic.

While open-minded people have firm ideas about how to operate their business, they do not write it off to luck or questionable business practices when they see a competitor succeeding ahead of them. They are eager to learn something new about themselves or their industry. Open-minded people also have firm convictions about politics. Since they know what they believe, they are not threatened by hearing what others believe. They are open to conversation and not distressed by new ideas or new information.

Open-minded people multiply their influence because they are open not just to new data, but also to new people. They are welcoming, attentive, and unruffled by new experiences. Because they have the self-confidence to listen and learn, they gain the respect of others, and their opinions take on even greater weight.

To become more open-minded, simply ask yourself this question when your mind wants to close against new information, new ideas, or new people: "What am I afraid of?" In nearly every case you'll find that there is no reason to fear the simple act of listening to what others have to say.

5. Possibility

The late pastor and author Robert Schuller coined the term *possibility thinking* to describe another aspect of positive thought. In contrast to those who see only negative outcomes—the "glass half-empty" thinkers—Schuller wrote, "The possibility thinkers perceptively probe every problem, proposal, and opportunity to discover the positive aspects present in almost every human situation. They are people—just like you—who when faced with a mountain do not quit. They keep on striving until they climb over, find a pass through, tunnel underneath—or simply stay and turn their mountain into a gold mine."[9]

Possibility thinking looks at every situation with this question in mind: "What good can I find in this?" This sort of thinking is exemplified in the line from George Bernard Shaw, famously quoted by Robert F. Kennedy, "Some people see things as they are and say why? I dream things that never were and say, why not?"[10] Possibility thinkers are convinced that a good outcome is possible no matter how difficult the situation may be. This goes beyond optimism—the idea that the worst possible result is unlikely—to probe for a positive outcome when disaster seems certain.

I love the joke about two boys who were twins, one a natural possibility thinker and the other a die-hard pessimist. The boys' parents noticed the difference in their temperaments and took them to a psychologist for evaluation. The doctor observed them and concluded that he could change their outlook and, therefore, their behavior.

The psychologist placed the pessimistic child in a room filled with all the toys any boy could want. He put the possibility thinker in a room filled with horse manure. "That should adjust their attitudes," he stated confidently. A video camera placed in each room allowed the doctor and parents to observe both children.

Contrary to all expectations, the pessimistic child continued to have a dour attitude, complaining that he had nobody to play with. Surrounded by all the good things in life, he continued to see the world in a negative light. Then the psychologist and parents looked in on the other child. They were amazed to find him digging through the manure. The psychologist ran into the room and asked what on earth the boy was doing. He said, "With all this manure, there's got to be a pony in there somewhere!"

Possibility thinkers are always influencers because people are always looking for fresh possibilities. Even negative thinkers long for a better world. They're just convinced no positive change is possible. If you can show others realistic prospects they have not yet seen, even confirmed pessimists will rally to your side. Everyone wants to believe in possibilities. Some are simply too tired, too worn down, and too defeated to imagine them for themselves.

6. Big Picture

The idea that positive thinkers are detached from reality is a standard criticism. Some would argue that positive thinkers go through life, seeing the blue skies ahead but never noticing the storm clouds on the horizon. All they can see is the forest, never the trees or the danger lurking among them. Positive thinkers simply aren't paying attention to the details, so the objection goes.

However, research indicates that people who are less concerned with details are actually happier and better able to function. A granular focus can actually interfere with our ability to do life. One researcher noted that people in a depressed mood are more likely to notice small changes in a person's facial expression and interpret them negatively, while happy people seem to overlook slight facial cues.[11] In other words, focusing on the trees to the point of being nitpicky can tend toward negative thinking and make you less effective. Positive-thinking people are more able to step back and see the forest. Granular thinking may be important from time to time, but big-picture thinking is essential to maintain a positive outlook and, therefore, to cast influence.

Do you tend to be a detail-oriented person or a big-picture thinker? There's nothing wrong with either, but you must be aware if your tendency is to focus on the minute details of a situation, as that can lead to paralysis. It's good to have some emotional intelligence, interpreting the social cues in a group of people. However, if you're constantly wondering, "What did she mean by that?" or "Why didn't he look up when I walked in?" you'll be paralyzed by anxiety.

It's okay to be the one asking about funding and budgets and how to make a project financially viable. But if you're always analyzing spreadsheets, you likely won't be inspired by the grand aims of the venture; you won't see what's possible.

Step back and look at the big picture. Be okay with not knowing every single detail. Trust others to do their job—whether in your home, workplace, or community—and shed the anxiety that inevitably comes with your desire for control. Even a detail thinker can look up at the sky occasionally. You don't have to count every star to be breathless at the sight of the heavens.

Big-picture thinkers are always more influential than those who see only the fine details. The abilities to envision a grand sweep of change and tolerate a bit of uncertainty are essential to leading others into the future. Yes, you must occasionally ask the hard questions about how all of this will work. But don't be afraid to think big.

7. Responsibility

A final aspect of positive thinking has to do with the freedom to make choices for yourself. Positive thinkers have a strong sense of *responsibility.* They believe that they have both the ability and the responsibility to take ownership of their own lives. They understand that they can and must think and act for themselves.

While that may sound obvious, it is anything but that to many people. Those with a negative outlook have been conditioned, sometimes by years of failure, to believe that they cannot improve their lives. They see themselves as victims, helpless at the hands of fate—or circumstances, or the economy, or giant corporations, or their family, or some other external force. Sadly, many come to have this victim mentality after years of abuse by others. Now they feel unable to move forward in life, even though their circumstances may have changed. They are not actors but reactors in their own lives.

I know that condition very well. I recall the pain, sadness, and frustration I felt at just 11 years of age when my father was killed in an industrial accident. Not well off to begin with, our working-class family was plunged into poverty. I carried a deep anger and a negative outlook well into my teenage years.

Fortunately, my college roommate, John C. Maxwell, and I were exposed to one of the great positive thinkers in the country during my freshman year of college. We attended a rally to hear Dr. Norman Vincent Peale, who had just authored the landmark book *The Power of Positive Thinking,* and other great motivators, including Zig Ziglar, Earl Nightingale, and W. Clement Stone. That rally marked the beginning of a profound change in me, for it was there that I discovered the incredible power of one's attitude upon behavior, happiness, future prospects, relationships—everything in life. It was the start of my life as a positive thinker, taking responsibility for my own choices.

Further, it was in a college chapel session two weeks later that I realized how positive thinking is fueled by faith. Immediately after hearing Roy S. Nicholson speak, I wrote these words in the front of my Bible: "A positive mental attitude without a positive faith will result in positive failure."

If you feel hopeless and helpless about your circumstances, I urge you to accept this fundamental truth: you have the power, with God's help, to choose your thoughts, your attitude, and your purpose in life.

While there may be circumstances around you that you cannot change, you can change the most important factor in your happiness. You can choose to take responsibility for your life.

If you struggle with a sense of helplessness about your future, practice repeating these twin truths to yourself: "I am responsible," and "I can." You are indeed responsible—not for what happens to you or around you, but for choosing your attitude and actions in response. That is something only you can do. Never surrender that power to another. You may not have the ability to change other people or to change certain circumstances in your life, but you can choose positive thoughts. You can choose to make changes in your own life. You can choose a different future than the one that has been handed to you.

People who exhibit and continually practice an inner strength are influencers because they have a strong sense of will and purpose, and that is always attractive to others. Those with a victim mind-set will remain stuck in life, unable to influence themselves or others. But those who understand that they are responsible to make their own choices will influence others to come along with them.

YOU CAN THINK POSITIVELY

For some, the prospect of adopting a positive mind-set is daunting. After years, or perhaps a lifetime, negative thought patterns become ingrained in the mind and emotions. You may think it's impossible to change your thoughts. But you can.

Begin by recognizing the negative thought patterns that have become part of your life. Notice when you are responding with pessimism, a scarcity mind-set, closed mindedness, or a victim mentality. Don't become discouraged or frustrated with yourself. Simply notice which types of negative thinking affect you most. Then you will know the areas in which you need to change.

Believe in yourself. Realize that you do have the ability and responsibility to take charge of your own mind. God created you as unique and gifted. Do not doubt that you can do this. Though it may take some time, you can become a positive thinker.

Seek accountability from a trusted friend or family member. Ask them to gently remind you of your resolve to be a positive thinker, and have them point out the instances when you slip into negativity. Share your journey with them and celebrate your success together.

And be persistent. When you recognize negative thinking within yourself, displace those thoughts and replace them with positive ones. Realize that you will have setbacks, but you will grow over time to become a positive thinker. Keep your goal in mind and do not become discouraged. You can do this!

Regardless of how negative your thinking may have been in the past, you can change. You can become a person whose thoughts and actions are characterized by optimism, humility, abundance, openness, possibility, magnitude, and responsibility. You can become a positive person. And when you do, you will influence those around you to be positive too. Remember, it all starts when you take control of your most valuable asset, your mind.

THE KEY THREE

1. Review the seven types of positive thinking and determine the ones in which you need to grow.

2. Name three practical steps you can take to become more positive in your thinking.

3. Enlist an accountability partner who will help you on your journey to become a positive thinker.

THE POWER OF
YOUR WORDS

*Words are a form of action, capable
of influencing change.*

–INGRID BENGIS[1]

A blind man sits on a city street. Beside him is a sign that reads "I'm blind, please help." All around him people are making their way through the streets, some laughing and chatting, others bored and distracted. Few notice the man, and only occasionally does anyone respond to his message. One or two people toss a small coin in his direction, which he eagerly gathers up and drops into a tin can by his side. Despite his pitiable condition and request for aid, almost no one notices or cares.

A well-dressed young woman happens by. She too walks past the man, then stops. She returns to regard the blind man and his circumstances. Without a word, she takes up his tattered cardboard sign, turns it over, and writes something on the other side. The blind man, aware that someone is nearby, reaches out to touch her stylish shoes. The woman replaces the sign and walks away.

Within moments passersby begin to notice the blind man. Most of them reach into their pockets to offer help. Coins now shower down about the man, who eagerly scoops them up, filling his tin can with money.

Sometime later, the young woman returns and stands before the man, smiling in approval. Sensing her presence, the man reaches out, feeling the same shoes as before. "What did you do to my sign?" he asks.

Kneeling down, the woman places a hand on his shoulder and says kindly, "I wrote the same, but different words." As she walks away, we see the sign as the woman recreated it:

"It's a beautiful day and I can't see it."[2]

This fictional story, conveyed in a brief video titled "The Power of Words," became an internet sensation for good reason. It shows the amazing power of words to influence the thoughts and actions of others. If you hope to influence others with your vision for the future, your positive thoughts must be translated into positive words. Your words have the power to change the world.

Words are the single most potent means of influence at your disposal. In this chapter, you will discover the incredible power contained within the simple words you speak every day. You'll learn how negative words undermine your influence in the world, and you'll find out how to use positive speech to deepen your impact on those around you.

WHY WORDS HAVE POWER

Words have great power in our lives because they shape how we perceive reality. Words do not have the power to create reality, but they do change how we understand it, and therefore how we feel about it and what we do about it. Words are the key to belief, and belief unlocks action.

For example, when you meet someone for the first time, a single word of introduction has the power to shape how you feel about that person and, therefore, how you respond to them. Have you ever met someone whom you'd heard described as untrustworthy, narcissistic, shallow, or uninteresting? What was your first reaction to them? Likely you were looking for signs to confirm the judgment you'd been given. Even if that description was untrue, it probably took a long time to dispel the notion. One negative word shaped your perception of the individual, making it nearly impossible to see their better qualities. In the same way, when you meet someone who is described as likable, friendly, or funny, you're almost certain to be receptive to them and give them the benefit of the doubt.

Words are the filter that reality must pass through to get into your brain. As such, they have tremendous power to shape how you think, feel, and behave.

It's no surprise, then, that politicians, activists, and marketers vie to define the terms surrounding any idea or product. When passing a law, it makes a huge difference whether the public perceives it as a "job killer" or a "deficit reducer." And we are much more likely to buy a product that is presented in terms of its benefits—chic, cutting edge, elegant, excellent—rather than its drawbacks—expensive, unnecessary, unproven.

Words have even greater power when applied to people. You've heard the old saying, "Sticks and stones may break my bones but names will never harm me." That adage focuses on the first part of our understanding of words: they do not create reality. A rock thrown in your direction may literally reshape a part of your anatomy, but a name, label, insult, or other word cannot affect your physical well-being; it can't change reality.

That's a nice thought, and it may help some folk to let insults roll off their backs. Yet anyone who has been on the receiving end of name calling or trolling will tell you that words applied to your spirit have the same effect as words applied to any other thing. The words cannot change your objective reality, but they can shape how you perceive yourself. Negative words really can cause psychological damage.

When you speak words, either positive or negative, they influence those around you to accept your view of reality. When you disparage an idea, others will think less of it, regardless of whether it is true or false. When you praise a product, others will be more inclined to try it, regardless of its objective benefits. In that sense, your words have tremendous power. They are a potent means of exercising influence over those around you.

To use your words as a means of influence, it's important to understand various kinds of speech—both positive and negative—and how they impact your ability to influence others. We'll begin by examining several forms of negative speech that you must learn to recognize and avoid.

NEGATIVE SPEECH THAT KILLS INFLUENCE

Most forms of negative speech are merely negative thinking expressed in words. They are your negative thoughts and formulations cast as the most rudimentary form of action—talking. Negative speech undermines your ability to influence others in two ways.

First, negative speech is always hostile either to a person or an idea. While it is legitimate and often helpful to offer a negative opinion—saying that something isn't true, for example, or that an idea is infeasible—negative speech often goes beyond that. It can become a kind of attack, often subtle, against another person. So negative speech is an influence killer because it sets you in opposition to the very people you might want to influence.

A second reason negative speech undermines influence is because speaking negatively easily becomes a habit, making you appear to others as a negative person. While it might be true that negative influence is still influence, it certainly is not the influence you want to exert on others. The hope you have for the world is positive. You want others to accept your vision for a better future in your family, workplace, or community. Negative speech may make you a destroyer, but it will never make you a builder.

To influence others in a positive direction, you must offer a hopeful, positive alternative to their current perception of reality—not simply undermine the way they currently think. Let's see how negativity kills your influence in these common forms of negative speech.

Complaining

Complaining is voicing displeasure over circumstances, particularly about things that are beyond your control. We are all tempted to complain about things (or people) whom we don't like. You cannot change the weather, so you complain that it's raining when you'd like to be out. You can't clear up a traffic jam, so you sit on the freeway and complain about being stuck. You cannot change the behavior of coworkers, so you voice a gripe to them and others.

Complaining feels good but is entirely counterproductive. It seems like a positive thing to do because it gets your frustration off your chest, relieving the annoyance temporarily. And it can be a bonding experience. When you complain, others will join you, making your aggravation a shared event.

The effects are short lived, however, and voicing complaints nearly always produces two negative effects in your life. First, it makes you feel worse in the long run by reinforcing the idea that you are helpless. Complaining about the rain does nothing to construct a positive plan for the day. It just makes you feel trapped in the house. Complaining about a coworker does nothing to address the problem. It merely makes you feel stuck in a situation you can't control. Far from improving your outlook, complaining actually makes you feel more frustrated.

Second, complaining reduces your ability to lead others in finding positive solutions. For one thing, you are far less likely to look for solutions when you trap yourself in a loop of negative thinking. Remember how negative thinking affects the brain. When you complain, you are far less likely to be able to think creatively and come up with solutions. Not only that, but complaining also casts you in a negative role among your peers. Family members, coworkers, and online friends may find humor in your complaints and even join you for a while, but they are unlikely to see you as a leader. Your ability to influence them in a positive direction will be severely compromised by your penchant for complaining.

Expressing Outrage

Outrage is a useful emotion when confronted with something truly outrageous. We do right to be outraged by genocide or the abuse of children or racial discrimination. However, the outrage that we most often hear expressed, especially on social media or other online forums, is something closer to the self-righteous condemnation of others. Outrage over gross evil is perfectly legitimate and necessary. But loudly condemning others for their mistakes, missteps, or errors in judgment while ignoring our own shortcomings is one of the most virulent forms of negative speech today.

As Jesus once said, it's the height of hypocrisy to take a speck of sawdust out of another person's eye when you have a two-by-four lodged in your own.[3] When you express rank indignation or outrage over what should be forgivable offenses, you undermine your influence by making yourself appear hypocritical. As with complaining, it's easy to aggregate a group of followers who are similarly indignant. But if you want to extend your influence, reserve your outrage for the truly outrageous. Be known as a person who is tolerant and fair minded.

Naysaying

Naysaying is devaluing an idea without giving it full consideration. You will hear it nearly anytime a change is proposed at work, school, church, or any other social structure. The two most popular statements of naysayers are "That'll never work" and "We've never done it that way before," with honorable mention going to "We tried that once and got nowhere."

Naysayers purport to be good leaders because, in their minds, they're trying to save everyone time. What they *think* they're saying is "Trust me, I have this one figured out." What people actually hear, however, is "You're not smart enough to think this through," which is a terribly negative message to give to others. Most often, what naysayers would say if they were being totally honest is something more like this: "I'm so afraid of change that I'm not even willing to consider what you're proposing."

Naysayers may be successful in winning an argument or controlling the decision making of a group, but that is a far cry from influence. Real influence is guiding people to a positive outcome that you have envisioned, not simply blocking others from implementing their ideas.

Criticizing

Criticizing is demeaning a person or idea without constructive intent. This is not the same as constructive advice, sometimes called constructive criticism (more on that later). What is meant here by criticism is tearing others down with no intention of building them up.

It's easy to be critical because other people—including you and me—have plenty of faults. We all make mistakes, do things imperfectly, overreact occasionally, and get wrong ideas. Almost everyone can see the faults and foibles in another person, so being critical is the easiest thing in the world to do. And it feels good. For some reason, we always feel as if we stand a little taller when we're standing on the rubble of another person's work, ideas, or reputation.

We don't, of course. And criticism is entirely detrimental to our ability to influence others. When you become known as a critic, people will look to you only when they want to hear the worst about a person, idea, or situation. But since they realize that your judgments are always negative, they will never trust you to provide the way forward.

Gossiping

Gossiping is criticizing someone who is not present. Gossiping may also be defined as repeating negative information about a person—whether true or untrue—without a definite need to do so. Privately warning a friend who is considering a business deal that the other party once swindled you is not gossip. The information is true and you have a definite need to share it privately. However, telling a group of friends that another person's marriage is breaking apart—so you've heard—is gossiping. The information may indeed be true, but when shared with no positive intent and to a wider circle than necessary, it becomes gossip. Gossip usually begins with the words, "I heard that . . ."

Nearly all negative information that cannot be verified may be considered gossip, regardless of the forum in which it is shared. By that definition, much of the news we read via social media might be considered gossip. To avoid gossiping, ask yourself these three questions:

1. Do I know for sure that this is true?
2. Do I have a constructive and compelling reason for repeating this information?
3. Am I sharing this information with the minimum number of people required to satisfy my reason for sharing?

If the answer to any of the three questions is no, sharing it with even one person is likely a form of gossip.

Gossiping, like complaining, is negative influence. It influences others *not* to trust, accept, or welcome another person, initiative, or idea. A person with a reputation for gossiping is generally considered untrustworthy, even by those who give ear to the gossip. Therefore, those who gossip are seldom able to influence others in positive ways. To protect your influence over others, avoid gossiping.

Trolling

Trolling is a new form of negative speech unique to online communication. It is faultfinding and gossiping in online media, particularly social media. Trolling is purposely destructive speech, often aimed directly toward another person. Trolls say negative—often hostile or nasty—things to or about others with no other purpose than to tear down their ideas or shame them.

Trolling is easy to do because of the relative distance that the internet provides (online versus face to face) and the shared outrage of a group or tribe. Sarcastic comments left on a blog, belittling jokes passed along through social media, and "gotcha" tweets and Facebook posts are all examples of trolling.

Trolls have great power to destroy but none to cast vision, influence positively, or provide leadership. If you hope to influence others, you cannot begin that leadership with sarcasm, mockery, or insults. To lead positively, communicate positively.

Spinning

The concept of *spin* has entered our vocabulary through politics, where a politician's surrogates or other pundits will amplify a speaker's remarks in order to "spin" them in a different direction. While it is legitimate to clarify a speaker's intention, the term *spin* has come to mean shading or distorting the truth by providing an alternative view of reality.

It isn't just politicians who spin the facts. A struggling business may spin their situation to a creditor by saying that they are "positioning themselves for success." A deceitful spouse may spin their behavior as "misremembering" what happened.

This old joke about a political candidate reveals the absurdity of trying to spin the truth. The politician said, "Half of my constituents are for this issue, and the other half of my constituents are against it. I want to make it absolutely clear to all that I am 100 percent behind my constituents!"

Most people are uncomfortable with telling outright lies, but untruthfulness comes in many lesser forms—such as exaggerating, omitting important facts, and making misleading statements. People who spin the truth seldom have influence outside their tribe. In other words, the only people they influence are those who already believe their ideas. If you want to cast wide influence, tell the truth, without embellishment, in all situations.

POSITIVE SPEECH THAT SHAPES INFLUENCE

Negative speech is an influence killer, but positive speech enhances reputation and builds influence. When you become a positive thinker, those positive thoughts will seep out through your words. As they do, you'll become known as a person who is affirming, open to others, and brimming with good ideas. You'll become an influencer. Here are several kinds of positive speech that will establish you as an influencer of others. While some are the direct opposites of the negative speech we just examined, many are unique forms of positive communication. Master these, and others will listen to you.

Making Positive Observations

Making positive observations is simply pointing out what's good, right, or hopeful in a situation. It is the opposite of complaining, which voices the negatives. Positive observations inspire hope and opportunity by identifying what's possible in any given situation. Rather than making you feel dour and helpless, positive observations build your spirit and create new possibilities.

For example, if it's raining on the day you planned to play golf, one reaction would be to complain about the weather, making you feel miserable and trapped. A positive observation could be to mention that it's a perfect day for reorganizing the basement.

When you're stuck in traffic, you can complain about the

inconvenience, making you and your companions tense and anxious, or you might observe that it's a great opportunity to finish your conversation or listen to an interesting podcast.

Making positive observations begins with asking the question, "What does this make possible?" when confronting a frustrating circumstance. If you think about it, there is nearly always some new opportunity hidden within a disappointment. Those who make positive observations are natural influencers, and their enthusiasm for new ideas gains them respect.

Complimenting

A compliment is a positive observation addressed to a person. It points out something good, right, or pleasing about them. It's the opposite of an insult. Notice, however, that there is an important difference between compliments and flattery. Flattery is false or inflated praise given for the purpose of influencing another person. You might flatter a person about their appearance, hoping they'll accept your invitation to dinner. Or you might flatter your boss's management ability, hoping she'll promote you or give you a raise. Flattery is always a bit exaggerated and always calculated for some ulterior purpose.

In contrast, compliments are honest, often spontaneous, and always free of charge. You compliment a coworker on his performance because you're honestly impressed. You compliment your spouse on their appearance because it is pleasing to you. You praise a child's growth or learning because you have a genuine desire to see them grow. A compliment must be sincere, and it must be offered without the hope of gaining something in return.

There is a saying that goes something like this: "Show me a man who doesn't like praise, and I'll show you a man who doesn't like anything." Those who are liberal with compliments are natural influencers because people crave honest praise about themselves. People have a difficult time seeing themselves accurately, and truthful, positive feedback is always welcome. But most people do have enough self-awareness to spot flattery. They know when they're being played, and they come to resent it. Those who give honest compliments are sought out and valued.

Be generous with complimenting others. It costs you nothing to observe the best in another person, and it gains trust, furthers relationships, and builds influence.

Giving Constructive Advice

Constructive advice is feedback or instruction given for the purpose of helping another person change, learn, or succeed. While some call this constructive criticism, I prefer the more positive term *advice*, because the word *criticism* has come to have an entirely negative connotation.

Constructive advice is easy to formulate but challenging to deliver well. Other people's gaps in learning or ability are always plain to see, so it's often very easy to understand where they need to grow. However, people are naturally defensive about themselves and their shortcomings, so advice in any form is often unwelcome. Following are some things to remember when giving constructive advice.

First, *the receiver must be open to it.* Avoid offering unsolicited advice, no matter how noble your motivation may be. Wait for the person to ask for your opinion, or gently offer to share your expertise. If there is no permission to share your advice, it will be unwelcome, and it will likely undermine your ability to influence the person further.

Second, *remember that hearing about your own failings, shortcomings, or need for improvement is difficult.* Be gentle, and always point your advice in a positive direction. I like to use the "sandwich method," placing constructive advice between two compliments. Here's an example: "Wow, I'm really impressed by how well you prepared for that presentation. Great job! Here is one idea that might help you deliver the material with greater impact. Again, I'm so impressed by the depth of information you shared." Hearing what they've done right always makes people more receptive to hearing how they could improve. And you can use this method in any setting, including with spouses, children, or neighbors.

Third, *check your motivation.* If your true desire is to vent irritation about a person's failings rather than to help them grow as a person, don't attempt to offer constructive advice. This is about the other person's growth and learning, not your frustration. Be sure that you're motivated by a genuine concern for others.

When given properly, constructive advice is a powerful form of positive speech. When you focus on others with the intention of helping them, it builds trust, respect, and influence.

Vision Casting

Vision casting is sharing your picture of the future with others in a way that inspires them to join you in creating it. This goes beyond making positive observations or finding the silver lining in a frustrating situation. Vision casting is defining a clear, positive vision for the future that excites the imagination of others and unlocks their motivation.

Many people confuse vision casting with goal setting, but the two are entirely different. Goals are specific, measurable, and time bound. They tell you exactly what you want to do next, and, in most contexts, you simply have to announce them, gain agreement, and then follow up to ensure they're achieved. "Paint the deck railing by the end of this month" is an example of a goal concerning home improvement.

Vision is different. It is a broad picture of an outcome, not a specific road map to achieving it. While a goal is a flat description of an achievement, a vision is an inspiring picture of the future. A vision for home improvement might be "to create an inviting, comfortable space for our family and friends."

Also, a goal can be created, posted, and reviewed occasionally to ensure progress. A vision must dwell within the mind, inspiring motivation nearly every day. A goal may be reviewed monthly or quarterly. A vision must be repeated over and over again until it becomes hardwired into one's thinking.

So vision casting must be done continually, especially in informal situations. Goals are announced at the annual meeting; vision is reinforced in casual conversation. Goals are placed on a spreadsheet; vision becomes part of your email signature. Goals often engender a sense of responsibility; vision creates possibility.

When you repeat your vision frequently, positively, and hopefully, you inspire others to join you in making it reality. In that sense, vision casting is the foundational form of influence. It is the positive speech that most directly affects the thoughts and actions of others.

Truth Telling

Truth telling is being honest in any given situation. It is the perfect blend of tact and candor, saying what is true in a helpful manner that neither conceals, withholds, nor harms others. It is the opposite of spinning, which presents a distorted or self-serving view of reality.

Providing correct information is an important part of truth telling, obviously. But as we saw with the discussion on spinning, it is possible to use or omit factual information in a way that misleads others. Honesty goes beyond factual accuracy to give a true presentation of reality. When you have 17,421 subscribers to your blog, you could spin that number by saying that you have "some 20,000 daily readers." Or you could, more truthfully, say that "about 17,000 people receive my posts by email." If you are 20 minutes late for an appointment, you could, perhaps accurately, state that you got held up by an accident on the highway. Or, knowing that the accident caused only a 10-minute delay, you might more honestly say, "I'm sorry I kept you waiting."

It's important to remember, however, that being honest is not a license for being rude. Some people confuse the two, dishing out truthful but insensitive comments with the disclaimer, "I'm just the sort of person who speaks their mind," or, "I tell the truth, and I don't care if you don't like it." Truth and tact are not mutually exclusive. While candid confrontation is sometimes necessary, it is nearly always possible to be honest and kind at the same time.

Here is the simple truth that those who get caught in the "spin zone" seem to forget: people find complete honesty refreshing, and they respect those who practice it. An ancient proverb holds that "an honest answer is like a kiss on the lips."[4] How true that is. In a world too often characterized by dishonesty and manipulation, it is pleasing to find an honest soul. That's why truthful people are always influential. When people realize that you are more committed to telling the truth than to protecting your ego or agenda, they will trust and respect you all the more.

Apologizing

An apology is an admission of truth regarding one's own failure, combined with a willingness to make amends. It is one of the rarest forms of positive speech because it requires deep humility. An apology requires a voluntary exposure of one's fault and places oneself at the mercy of another. It is risky and threatening, which is why so many people avoid apologizing.

As alternatives to offering an apology, we often resort to defensive tactics such as ignoring, rationalizing, or blaming. We may pretend that we've done nothing wrong or that no breach in a relationship has occurred. "Problem? What problem?" we say, refusing to acknowledge what happened. Or we may invent reasons why our behavior was necessary or why we are not truly at fault. We say things like, "It's not my fault; I was really tired," or "How was I supposed to know the project was due yesterday?" Worse, we may blame others, even the person we've wronged. We may throw around accusations such as, "She started it," or "If you had been on time, none of this would have happened." Such tactics only make the situation worse. They deepen the rifts in our relationships with others and undermine our influence.

To apologize is simply to admit the truth and offer to make amends. "I'm sorry I said that. I was in the wrong, and I'd like to make it up to you." "I didn't see the car parked there, and that was careless of me. I'm sorry about that, and I'm going to notify my insurance company right away."

When you are at fault in any situation, you gain respect and credibility by admitting the truth. Apart from being the right thing to do—which it always is when you are in the wrong—apologizing builds your influence over others because they come to see that you are truthful, even about yourself.

START THE CYCLE

If you still doubt the power of positive words, consider this letter, which appeared some years ago in an advice column in the *Chicago Tribune*.

In August of 1991, I was told I had brain cancer and my chances of living another five years were at best 50-50. When word of this leaked to my friends, two of them began a letter- and card-writing campaign. All the pilots employed by our airline got involved.

The response was overwhelming. I received stacks of cards and letters every day. The doctors and nurses also let me know they were interested in my recovery and gave me a lot of T.L.C. The all-female team in the radiation department where I took my treatment deserves special mention for its perpetual smiles and supportive attitude. My pilot buddies collected enough money to send me and my family to Disney World for a beautiful vacation.

Surrounded by all that love, I couldn't help but get better. I am now classified as a cancer survivor, and the support of my friends continues to this day. I am convinced that "friend therapy" can be a big factor in recovery.

To all those incredible people who helped me in my time of need, I say thank you and may God bless you.

Robert Berry, Shreveport, La.

Columnist Ann Landers responded: "While I am not suggesting that positive thinking can cure cancer, there is a great deal of evidence that the immune system does respond to what goes on in the brain. Thanks for a real upper. I'm sure you've spread a lot of joy today."[5]

Your words can have a dramatic, positive effect on those around you. Though your words may not have the power to cure cancer, your encouragement will speed and support the recovery of those afflicted. Your words cannot single-handedly transform the entire internet, but your gentleness and honesty can be a beacon of hope to those mired in manipulation and negativity. Your words cannot change reality, but they can inspire those around you to change it for themselves.

Positive thoughts beget positive words. And your positive words can reframe a negative situation, encourage a dispirited person, and point to a positive future. Your words do indeed have power. Use them well.

THE KEY THREE

1. Take mental inventory of your speech patterns for the past 24 hours. Note your use of both positive and negative words, and identify the trigger moments for each.

2. Name one form of negative speech you intend to eliminate, and one form of positive speech you intend to cultivate.

3. Choose one person in your home, school, or workplace and ask them to hold you accountable to use your words in a positive manner.

THE POWER OF YOUR EXAMPLE

*If you would convince a man that he does wrong,
do right. But do not care to convince him. Men
will believe what they see. Let them see.*

HENRY DAVID THOREAU[1]

According to legend, a monk named Brother Leo was known for his incomparable leadership at a particular monastery in France. The holy man was regarded as such a great leader that his reputation spread all over Europe. Other monks would make pilgrimages to France to learn from this extraordinary man. On one occasion, a group of monks set out to visit Brother Leo, but on the way they began to argue over who was responsible for doing the group's chores.

On the third day of their journey they met another monk on his way to the same monastery, and he joined their group. This monk never argued about chores and did them willingly. When the others would bicker about whose turn it was to cook or clean up, he would simply get up and do the task himself. After several days, the others began to follow this patient monk's example, and the bickering came to an end.

At last they reached their destination, and the traveling monks announced the purpose of their visit. "We would like to meet Brother Leo," they told the man who greeted them.

"But our brother is among you!" the man replied, pointing to the patient monk who had joined them on their journey.

Your example is the silent influence you have over others, even when you are not aware of it. People observe what you do to an even greater degree than they heed your words. Positive thoughts produce positive words, and both should produce positive behavior in you. That consistent example—embodying the change you want to see in the world—will place a seal upon your words, giving them even greater power.

In this chapter, we will review the basic truth that actions speak louder than words. We will then dig deeper on that concept to understand how your example actually influences others. And finally, we will explore the factors that limit your positive example and discover how you can cultivate a consistently strong influence through your habits and actions.

WHY YOUR EXAMPLE MATTERS

Do your actions have any bearing on your influence, or are results the only thing that matters? As incredible as it may seem, our culture is engaged in a debate right now about that very question. What was once accepted as a bedrock principle of leadership—"character counts"—is now being dismissed as a quaint archaism. In politics, business, and even the church, it appears that we are more and more willing to tolerate those who say one thing and do another, so long as they are able to bring about the outcome we hope for.

Yet it is a grave mistake for anyone to think they can escape the character question for long. High-profile leaders, entertainers, or athletes may be given more grace in this area while they are in their prime. But a fickle public will quickly indict those character flaws when the heroes stop winning, making money, or producing hits. For ordinary folks like you and me, character always has been and always will be an essential component of influence. People follow those whom they trust, and nothing builds trust better than a good example. Here are four reasons your positive example is essential to influencing others.

1. Your example sets the tone that others will follow.

As in the story of Brother Leo, example exerts a silent, powerful influence over others. When the example is consistent, people will naturally begin to align themselves with it. This is true of many behaviors, even in humorous ways. When you smile, people will smile back. When you laugh, others will join you in laughing. And a yawn is one of the most contagious of all human behaviors. It's possible that you had to stifle the urge to yawn after simply reading the word. Scientists now believe that yawning is contagious because of our innate desire to bond with others through shared experience. The urge is so powerful that one study found that even dogs will join in more than 70 percent of the time.[2] Your example matters because people who are close to you will have a natural tendency to copy your behavior, whether good or bad. Your actions influence others to follow.

2. Your example models what you are trying to accomplish.

Example is a great, natural teaching tool. As the old saying goes, "A picture is worth a thousand words." Brother Leo could have lectured the monks about volunteerism or having a gentle spirit, but his example communicated those traits more effectively than any speech could have done. When you greet customers with a smile and welcome, others will see how to offer good service. When you load the dishwasher properly, others will understand how to get the dishes cleaner. When you show up for work on time and quit at a reasonable hour, other people learn how to structure a daily routine. Another adage puts it this way: "Tell me and I will forget. Show me and I will remember."

3. Your example raises others' sights, helping them see what's possible for themselves and the world.

I've never been a great golfer, but I enjoy a round from time to time. Years ago, when I was learning to play, I thought the game was impossible. I simply could not hit the ball straight down the fairway; my slice was legendary. I was ready to give up the game altogether. Then one day I saw the club pro at our local course step up to the first tee. He stretched briefly, teed the ball, then let his club come to rest just behind it. In a flash, he drew back the club and unleashed the quickest, most powerful stroke I'd ever seen, turning his body into a veritable corkscrew with his follow through. With a satisfying *thwack,* the ball erupted from the tee and flew high, straight, and long, coming to rest well over 250 yards down the middle of the fairway.

"So *that's* how it's done," I said to myself. Though I've never achieved that level of mastery, that single shot gave me a new perspective on the game of golf. I began to see what was possible and resolved to keep trying.

Your example can have that same influence over others in whatever arena you're working. When you forgive someone who has wronged you, others will see it's possible to forgive. When you resist gossip, profanity, or other forms of negative speech, others will see they can too. When you achieve financial freedom by avoiding debt and investing money, your example becomes a beacon for others to follow. Many people simply don't know (or can't make themselves believe) that a different life is possible for them. Your example can raise their sights and give them hope.

4. Your example keeps you involved in your own vision.

It is frightfully easy to make resolutions for yourself, your family, or others, and never follow through on them. You've experienced this, no doubt, when starting a budget, determining to get in better physical shape, or resolving, "This year, we're going to plant a garden!" That's easy to say in February, but by May your attention may have turned to other things.

When you set a positive example for others, you keep yourself engaged in the work you're trying to accomplish. In fact, you influence yourself. When you are mindful to put your cell phone down when behind the wheel, you show your kids something important about safe driving—and you also reinforce your own desire to protect your family. When you take a walk at lunchtime rather than heading straight back to your desk, you set an example of physical fitness for others to follow—and you also reinforce your own desire to have an active lifestyle. Your positive example benefits others, to be sure. But it benefits you even more.

Setting a good example is easier said than done, however. Even those with good intentions occasionally find themselves influencing others in the wrong direction by their actions (or inaction). Let's talk about some example killers and how to avoid them.

EXAMPLE KILLERS

As mentioned earlier, a saying attributed to famed investor Warren Buffett holds that "it takes twenty years to build a reputation and five minutes to ruin it."[3] The same could be said of your good example—and the influence that goes with it. Past instances of this sort of failure are too easy to recall. Everyone can remember a case of a politician whose example of public service was negated by self-serving financial dealings, or a religious leader whose moral example was contradicted by scandal. When such things happen, the damage often extends well beyond the incident at hand. Skeptical onlookers may in the future gaze askance at any examples of altruism or decency, figuring that nobody is able to "practice what they preach."

The lesson here is that you can be your own worst enemy in the area of displaying a positive example. When you contradict your own good words and intentions through thoughtless, foolish, or selfish actions, the damage to your influence can be irreparable. That makes it essential to understand the three most common example killers. When you understand them and how they can creep into your life, you'll be able to avoid them, preserving the influence of your good example.

Hypocrisy

The first example killer is *hypocrisy*. Hypocrisy is giving the appearance of having a virtuous character or point of view that you don't really possess. Everyone abhors hypocrisy, but it's relatively easy to slip into because we all aspire to ideals that we have not yet fully achieved. You value truthfulness, so you may loudly, and genuinely, decry dishonesty in others. Yet when you come under pressure, you are tempted to exaggerate, report false numbers, or tell a "white lie." Few people set out to be hypocrites, but most of us end up behaving hypocritically at some point in our lives.

Hypocrisy is toxic to influence precisely because people are so finely attuned to it. Honest mistakes are easy to overlook, but when someone appears to be dealing falsely by pretending to be something they're not, it arouses deep anger. Even a hint of hypocrisy will be harmful to your influence.

To avoid hypocrisy, you must do more than meet the minimum standard of integrity or truthfulness. You must set an example of good character. Don't simply recall facts to the best of your ability. Ensure that you communicate an accurate understanding of the truth, without embellishment or omission. Don't simply report your expenses accurately; give the benefit of the doubt to your employer by not claiming any expense that might push the boundaries of the company's policy. Practice what you preach. Treat others as you'd like to be treated. Go out of your way to avoid the appearance of being hypocritical. The higher your integrity, the greater your influence. A single drop of hypocrisy can taint your example for years to come.

Inconsistency

The second example killer is *inconsistency*. In terms of your example, inconsistency is setting a good example at some times but not others. It is a lack of constancy or dependability in modeling your vision for the world.

Setting an inconsistent example merely frustrates others because they come to think they can't count on you. You may be the first one to the team meeting one day, brimming with good ideas and full of enthusiasm. That attitude and action set a good example, and others may begin to look to you as a leader. But when you show up tired and irritable the next week, eyes glued to your phone and grunting one-word answers, they will quickly conclude that you're not serious about making an impact. The next time you try to rally the troops, no one will listen. They'll believe that you don't mean it or won't follow through.

Consistency is vitally important in influencing anyone—from coworkers, to family members, to neighbors and friends. When they see you behave the same way all the time, regardless of the circumstances, your example will be highly influential.

Arrogance

The third example killer is *arrogance*. Arrogance is a feeling of superiority that reveals itself through a prideful or condescending attitude. Arrogance can be real or imagined. In other words, it doesn't matter whether you actually *feel* superior to others or not; when people perceive that you do, it will undermine your example. Nobody likes to be looked down upon, so people will not respond to an arrogant person regardless of whether or not they set a positive example in other ways.

When you are setting a good example and you know it, it can be difficult to avoid feeling self-righteous or superior. You may have observed this in others, or perhaps felt the tendency yourself. When you begin to take control of your health by exercising properly and eating wholesome foods, it can be tempting to be judgmental of those who still reach for the Twinkies and plop down on the couch. When you are diligent in getting enough sleep so you can arrive for class or work refreshed and ready to go, it's tempting to roll your eyes at those who shuffle in five minutes late, unprepared for the day. Ironically, it is your own good example that makes it possible for you to feel arrogance—which undermines your example!

To combat the tendency to be arrogant or judgmental, remember a couple of things: First, the people whom you are tempted to judge are the very ones you are trying to influence. Rather than focusing on their poor habits, think about the needs they face and how much it would help them to adopt better habits, as you've done. Think about how their behavior hurts them, not how it affects you. When you do, you'll feel compassionate toward others, not judgmental. Second, remember that you too have weaknesses and blind spots. A good dose of humility is a great cure for arrogance. Though you may set a good example in some areas, there are probably others in which you need more discipline. Each of us is a work in progress, so respond to others with kindness. The same standard you use in dealing with them will likely be used on you someday. Opt for gentleness every time.

Don't allow an attitude of superiority to creep into your heart, regardless of how much progress you have made. Remember that you struggled to get where you are. Avoid pointing to yourself as a good example. Never hold up others as a bad example. Let your actions speak louder than your words, and others will see that you have something good to offer them.

EXAMPLE BUILDERS

Hypocrisy, inconsistency, and arrogance are influence killers. They undermine your good example, destroying whatever positive influence your silent actions might otherwise have had. It's also true that there are example builders. Obviously, integrity, consistency, and humility—the direct opposites of influence killers—help to build your good example. Beyond these, however, here are a couple of practices you can incorporate into your life to strengthen your ability of setting a positive example.

State Your Motivation

Poor motivation is the primary cause of inconsistent performance. If you are setting an inconsistent example, it's not necessarily because you lack discipline. It's more likely that you yourself are unconvinced of the importance of what you're doing. That lack of conviction makes it all too easy for your attention to be drawn elsewhere, or for you to back off when discipline is required. But when you are convinced tomorrow's meeting is important, you'll turn off the TV and get to bed early. When you are fully committed to getting out of debt, you'll pass up impulse purchases at the checkout counter.

To solidify your good example, check your motivation. Refer to your vision—the change you'd like to see in yourself, your family, or the world around you. Remind yourself why this matters so much. Keep those thoughts in your mind by reviewing them daily. When you do this, the sine wave of up-and-down behavior will flatten into a steady pattern of achievement.

Create Strong Habits

Habits are like the operating system of the mind: the thoughts, attitudes, and actions that drive daily life. Many people are unaware of their own negative patterns and how those patterns sabotage achievement and happiness. However, when you create strong, positive habits, you set yourself up for success. Your positive example becomes automatic because it stems from actions you no longer think about taking.

To understand how habits become automatic, requiring no thought, consider something you do every single day. Regardless of whether or not you think of yourself as a highly structured person, you probably have some daily habits such as brushing your teeth, feeding the dog, or locking the door before you go to bed. Now, think for a minute: Did you do that yesterday? Do you remember brushing your teeth? Are you sure you fed the dog? Can you be positive that you locked the door? Probably not. It's likely you have no recollection of doing those things because you do them without making a conscious choice. They have become automatic.

When you automate positive behaviors by making them habits, you improve your lifestyle and make it more likely that you will create a positive example in your personal life, work, education, or anything you do. Following are a few positive habits you might consider adopting.

Bedtime and Waking Routines

Consider adopting a standard bedtime. When you go to bed at the same time each day, you're more likely to wake up fresh and well rested, thus better able to navigate your day. You'll be more likely to keep a positive attitude, work energetically, and set a good example in all you do.

Also, create habitual routines around going to bed and waking, involving things like shutting down your computer, brushing your teeth, praying and meditating, arranging clothes for the next day, packing a lunch, and stretching or exercising. These routines will help you sleep more soundly and start your day with greater energy.

Work Startup and Shutdown Routines

Many people become inconsistent in their work performance—or in setting a positive example in the workplace—because they begin their day 15 minutes behind schedule and never catch up. One reason for this is they lack consistent workday routines. Arriving for work at the same time every day, avoiding checking social media when your computer starts up, working from a preplanned agenda, and doing routine tasks in a given order will help you dive into work in a relaxed, confident manner.

It also helps to end work with a shutdown ritual, rather than walking out of the office with your inbox full and the message light blinking on your phone. Establish a routine that closes out one day's business and lays the groundwork for tomorrow. That'll help you move through each day with confidence and control, setting a good example for others.

Physical Habits

Proper diet and exercise are much touted because of their value to one's appearance. We all want to look good. But good health habits help you set an example as well. When you appear fit and energetic, people are more apt to follow your lead. And being healthier results in having more energy, accomplishing more, and having improved discipline in other areas of life.

Establish strong habits around healthy eating, physical flexibility, strength, and aerobic fitness. This is more than simply starting the latest fad diet or joining a gym. It is creating habits around nutrition and fitness that add up to a healthier, more active lifestyle. Your physical disciplines will enhance your ability to set a good example in attitude, work ethic, productivity, and other areas as well.

Mental and Spiritual Habits

It's been said that there are no weak people, only weak minds. If that is true, then establishing intellectual and spiritual habits will strengthen other areas of your life and assist you in setting a positive example. For me, those habits include reading for at least an hour a day, plus daily time for prayer and Scripture study. Your habits may differ, but don't neglect this area of your life. When life gets hectic, it's very difficult to "find time" for activities like reading, studying, deep thought, or meditation. That's why you must do them habitually, just like eating or bathing. Make your personal-growth habits a regular feature of your life.

The numbers vary from one expert to another, but it's said that it can take anywhere from three to six weeks to establish a habit. After that, it's yours for life. Take a few minutes to think about the habits you'd like to add to your daily or weekly routine, and which you would like to drop. Chances are good that you have one or two bad habits that infringe on your ability to set a good example. Habits like binge eating or drinking, excessive television watching or social media use, or frivolous spending actually work against your desire to influence others with your silent example. The sooner you eliminate them, the better.

BEING REAL

When you have a strong motivation to influence change and establish healthy routines in your life, you are likely to set a positive example. Seeing your passion and self-discipline, others will be drawn to you and begin to adopt your behaviors, just as the monks did in the legend about Brother Leo. Remember, though, that influence killers abound. You can easily sabotage your good example through hypocrisy, inconsistency, or arrogance.

That reminds me of a joke Melvin Maxwell told me about a man who went to the zoo in search of work. This man was willing to clean cages, feed animals, or do just about anything.

When the manager saw that the man was stockily built, he said, "I do have one job you might do. Our gorilla died last week, and we don't have a replacement. We do have a gorilla suit though. I'll hire you to wear the suit and impersonate the gorilla until his replacement arrives."

"I'll do it," the man said.

The next day, he arrived for work and was fitted with the suit. All morning long, he stomped around the gorilla enclosure, beating his chest, shaking the bars, and swinging on vines in front of the crowd. The audience loved it. But the man got so excited that he swung too high and landed himself over the fence in the lion enclosure.

Immediately, a large male lion strode toward the man in the gorilla suit. Realizing that any move on his part would give away the deception, he tried to keep his mouth shut. But as the lion approached, fear overwhelmed him and he cried out, "Help!"

Just then, he heard the lion speak as well. "Shh!" he whispered. "Keep your mouth shut or you'll get us both fired!"

Far too many people cruise through life pretending to be something they are not. Though they may be successful in gaining attention for a while, that influence will be short lived. It is difficult to keep up the pretense for long, and their true character inevitably comes forth in their words and actions. You simply cannot fake a good example.

However, when your motivation is genuine and your discipline is strong, your positive actions can become a source of inspiration and encouragement to the people around you. You can change the world without saying a word through the power of your good example.

THE KEY THREE

1. State your motivation for change. Say out loud why it matters so much to you that you influence others in the area you have chosen.

2. Name one bad habit you would like to eliminate from your life in order to strengthen your example.

3. Name one good habit that you will acquire to reinforce the example you hope to provide.

7

THE POWER OF
YOUR PRESENCE

*The further you go in life, the more you realize what
you're going to leave this earth. It's not going to
be, "It was a great platform. It was great to win the
Super Bowl," but really and truly what you're going
to leave on this earth is the influence on others.*

JOE GIBBS[1]

believe in the power of presence," said Debbie Hall, a psychologist in
San Diego's Naval Medical Center and a volunteer for the Disaster
Mental Health Team of her local Red Cross chapter. Hall discovered a
powerful lesson on the power of presence while working in the wake of
Hurricane Katrina. She said, "I and several other Red Cross volunteers
met a group of evacuees…. We were there, as mental health professionals, to offer 'psychological first aid.' Despite all the training in how to
'debrief,' to educate about stress reactions and to screen for those needing
therapy, I was struck again by the simple healing power of presence. Even
as we walked in the gate to the shelter, we were greeted with an ardent
burst of gratitude from the first person we encountered. I felt appreciated, but vaguely guilty, because I hadn't really done anything yet."[2]

The response Hall received is not unusual from victims of disaster
or trauma. My good friend Jo Anne Lyon, founder of the aid organization World Hope International, encountered the same phenomenon
when visiting West Africa at the height of Sierra Leone's civil war. She
described that experience in her book *The Ultimate Blessing*, in which
she discusses meeting an elderly refugee:

She was a small woman, and very frail. Her son told me that she was one hundred years of age, and I had no doubt of it. Family members had carried her for miles through the rugged bush country of Sierra Leone to the safety of a refugee camp in Kalia, Guinea. She was hunched over and walked only with assistance. Leaning on her son's arm, she approached me slowly as if to speak. Her voice was weak. I leaned down and listened as she whispered hoarsely, "Thank you. Thank you for being here. I thought we had been forgotten."[3]

In both these cases, the responses these women received weren't offered because they had brought extraordinary help, gifts of cash, a supply of medicine, or any other tangible benefit. They just showed up. They were present. And that simple fact produced a great blessing and an overwhelming sense of gratitude in the beleaguered people they met.

The effect of your presence is real and important, even in ordinary life. It isn't just disaster victims who need the presence of others. We are all communal beings, and it's important for us to be in the company of others. That makes your presence one of the greatest gifts you can give to another person, and one of the key elements of your influence in the world.

Woody Allen is noted as saying, "Showing up is 80 percent of life."[4] You can make a tremendous difference in the lives of others by being there. Beyond the things you say or do, your presence is the impact you have on others simply by being in the room. It is the sum of a number of subtle factors, including demeanor, manner of speech, facial expression, energy level, and behavior—but the most important aspect of your presence is simply being there.

In this chapter, you will come to see the often-underestimated effect of your presence on others, and you will discover strategies for changing "the temperature of the room" just by walking into it. You will learn how being who you are, right where you are, is one of the subtlest, most powerful ways to influence others.

WHAT PRESENCE IS

Your presence is tangible in the sense that you are a real, flesh-and-blood person who takes up physical space. You have a material presence wherever you go. But the concept of presence goes well beyond the cubic inches you occupy. Your presence is the intangible effect you have on others merely by being there. In that sense, presence is difficult to define. But you know it when you see it or, perhaps more accurately, when you feel it. Your presence is like a fragrance that precedes you into a space, having a subtle effect on those whom you contact and lingering after you are gone. Your presence changes how people feel and respond in any given situation.

If that sounds a bit vague, it may help to think of your favorite movie actor. Powerful performers like Tom Cruise, Nicole Kidman, Denzel Washington, and Angelina Jolie can electrify a scene just by walking onto the set. Love them or hate them, most people cannot help but watch them. They dominate the attention of the audience, often without saying a word.

While we may not be movie stars, we too have presence. We all communicate something when we walk into a room—and sometimes when we leave it. The simple fact of being present says something to others, as does the fact of being absent. Beyond that, our expressions, energy, eye contact, posture, and many other silent signals communicate to those around us, even when we appear to be doing nothing at all.

Presence may seem a bit like *example*, which we looked at in the previous chapter, but it is quite different. Your example is set by the positive things you do to provide a model, instruction, or motivation for others. Your presence, on the other hand, is not your actions or words. It is *you*, who you are and how you comport yourself in a given situation. This comparison chart may help clarify the difference between example and presence.

Example Says…	Presence Says…
"Here's what I'm doing."	"Here I am."
"Follow me."	"Be with me."
"This is how it's done."	"This is who I am."
"Let me show you."	"I'm here for you."

When you take an action that models good behavior for others, you're using the power of your example. When you simply choose to be yourself in a social context, you're exercising presence.

The power of presence is strong and meaningful, though it is indirect. Your words, especially your persuasive words, exert a direct influence on others. Your example is a less direct form of influence, but it still produces a result. People will follow your example and do what you do. But your presence influences others by enhancing their admiration and respect for you personally. It sets a mood or tone for the interactions that follow.

While it may sound calculating or manipulative to talk about the value of your presence in influencing others, it's actually a very meaningful and important part of your relationship with them. Medical and spiritual caregivers have long understood the tremendous importance of presence for healing and growth. When a nurse visits someone's bedside and places a hand on the patient's shoulder, it is an act of presence. That simple human contact also makes the patient more willing to follow the nurse's instructions, speeding recovery. Visiting a funeral home to comfort a widow is also an act of presence, even if no words are exchanged. Just being in the room is important. Presence is what makes it possible for the minister to later speak words that promote forgiveness, healing, and recovery.

If you want to lead people in the moment, like a military commander, use words. If you want to influence people to change short-term behavior, add the power of your example. But if you sincerely hope to gain the trust of others so that you can influence them over a lifetime, you must be present with them.

CREATING A POSITIVE PRESENCE

How do you create a positive presence? Do you simply show up when invited, and possibly smile more? Given that presence is an intangible quality that flows from your unique personality, outlook, and characteristics, is it even possible to alter your presence? What if your presence has a negative effect on others? Can you change that?

The elements of presence are difficult to pin down, but it is possible both to identify them and to change them in yourself. With a bit of thought and intentionality, you can exert a positive influence on others through your presence, even if you've had a negative effect in the past. Following are several elements of presence, along with some guidelines for improving the effect of your presence.

Self-Awareness

The first element of presence is self-awareness. You must be aware that you do in fact have a presence, and you must become aware of how that presence affects others. Most people are totally unaware of the fact that they affect others by being in a room, nor do they understand what that effect is. To exert a positive influence on others, you must give attention to both.

"Who, me?" That's the typical response you will hear when you point out the effect of a person's presence. For example, when a team member is sullen and silent, moodily sucking the life out of a meeting by refusing to comment or make eye contact, they will nearly always express surprise when challenged. "But I wasn't doing anything!" they'll protest. And they'll be right. However, it's possible to exert a negative presence with few or no overt actions. Though the person may be unaware of their presence, others will be acutely aware of how that person's demeanor affects the team.

Likewise, when you compliment a student on being a leader in the classroom, they may be taken off guard. They simply don't realize that being cheerful, being on time, making eye contact, and smiling all exert a powerful influence on those around them.

Everyone has a presence, though some may have a stronger presence than others. You may have a family member, friend, or coworker who dominates every social setting without really trying. When they smile, everyone else does too. When they decide to skip a meeting, most team members also fail to show. Others have a less intense effect on others. They may be overlooked at first, and they likely feel that nobody would notice if they were there or not. Not so. Each of us has some effect on others through the simple act of being present or absent and through the demeanor with which we present ourselves.

It's helpful to think of presence as a fragrance. When you wear perfume or cologne, you probably can't smell it, but others can. It's the same with foul odors. If you've been working in the barn all day, you can no longer smell the manure. But show up for dinner without changing your clothes, and the whole family will remind you: "Ew! Take a shower!"

So the first step to improving your presence is to be aware that you have one. Every day, wherever you go, you exert some influence on every person you meet. And remember, presence can be positive or negative. Some people make others uneasy by their presence, while some put others at ease. Some exude tension; some bring a sense of calm. Some appear weary and disorganized, while some bring a sense of energy and confidence.

What is your effect on others? Is it positive or negative?

That's a key question to ask yourself about presence. To continue the fragrance analogy, just like you can't smell yourself, how will you know what your presence is like? How do others perceive you? Here are a couple of ways to find out.

1. OBSERVE HOW OTHERS RESPOND TO YOU WHEN YOU ARE PRESENT.

Do all eyes focus on you when you enter a room? When a decision must be made, do people stop and look toward you? If so, you likely have a very strong presence. If not, don't be self-conscious. There are no bonus points for having a strong presence—only for having a *positive* one. If people are less likely to respond to you in a social setting, it probably means that you have a milder presence, and that's fine.

2. ASK ONE OR TWO PEOPLE WHOM YOU TRUST.

This may be challenging, and you must be prepared to receive what you hear without becoming defensive. You might ask questions like, "Do you think I tend to warm up a room when I enter, or shut it down?" Or, "On a scale of one to ten, how would you say I affect the people around me, if one is completely negative and ten is completely positive?" You might ask a couple of follow-up questions to help you understand the response.

Regardless of your starting point, you can make your presence more positive. Exploring the following aspects of presence will help you sort that out.

A Focus on Others

Having just stated that the first element of improving your presence is to be self-aware, the next element may seem to be a contradiction. However, to increase the impact of your presence, you must forget about yourself and focus on others. Remember, your influence is not about you. Your purpose is to improve your home, workplace, community, or other social context by making positive change. And to do that, you must be focused on the needs of other people, not yourself.

One of the key factors that contributes to a negative presence is self-centeredness. When people are selfish—either in general, or when they are simply self-absorbed in a given moment—they suck attention away from others. Even when they are silent, their sullenness communicates loudly, "I'm not happy!" or "I'm not getting what I need!" Being late, not giving attention to others, failing to make eye contact, not listening, appearing to be bored or distracted: all these things communicate that you feel you are more important than other people, and that's a terribly negative impression to give. It deflates the mood at a dinner table or in a classroom, conference room, or living room.

On the other hand, when you are able to put your needs aside temporarily and focus on other people, you communicate just the opposite. You show them through your presence that they are important, you are with them, and you are fully engaged in whatever is happening. You do that, first of all, by being present in the first place. You also communicate a positive presence by simple behaviors like being on time, listening, taking part in what's happening, making eye contact, and smiling. Notice what others are doing and saying. Respond when appropriate. Don't follow every remark in a conversation with a comment about yourself. Ask questions. Be interested in other people and what they need.

When you enter a hospital room, a quiet presence is essential. In a business meeting, an alert, engaged demeanor is appropriate. In every social context, ask yourself, "What's happening here? What do others need? How can I take part?" When you focus on others rather than yourself, you will create a positive presence that will be most welcome.

Intentional Presence or Absence

Imagine yourself in this situation: A coworker's grandmother passes away. You know your coworker well enough to know her grandmother was very important in her life, but you never met the woman yourself. You have a casual but growing relationship with your coworker, though you don't know anyone else in her family. She mentions that visiting hours at the funeral home will be tomorrow evening. You wonder, "Should I go?"

That question exposes the next aspect of presence, which is to be intentionally present—or absent—when appropriate. The difficulty, of course, is that it's sometimes hard to know which is best. Though there is no infallible guide for making such decisions, you should consider being present when

- your presence is expected by social convention;

- it is required by your school, employer, or other organization to which you belong, even if it is inconvenient for you; or

- being there would bring cheer or comfort, even though it's not required or expected.

Being present shows respect and demonstrates your willingness to put others first. A weekly team meeting may be boring, and you can certainly ask your employer to alter the meeting or excuse you. But it's disrespectful to others to simply not show up. And attending your neighbor's graduation may not be expected or required, but doing so could be a nice way to signal your concern and interest in the relationship.

Remember that presence alone is a powerful communicator. The simple act of attending a meeting, visiting a nursing home, showing up at a Little League game, or dropping by an open house is a positive, respectful sign that says, "You matter." Your presence is a gift: the gift of yourself. That gift is nearly always an honor to receive.

When you choose to be present, be intentional—not just in the choice to be there, but in how you comport yourself throughout the event. Be on time. Dress appropriately. Engage with those who are present. Don't duck out early without good reason. Wherever you are, be all there.

Likewise, be intentionally absent when appropriate. There are some occasions when your presence is not needed, would not be entirely welcome, or might hinder whatever is taking place. It may be more appropriate to stay away in such cases. For example, consider not being present when

- your presence would create awkward tension, even if you might have a right to attend;
- your absence might allow others to grow by letting them have a chance to lead or make decisions; or
- your absence may not be noted, but attending would place a burden on you or your family.

You may have a strong interest in the outcome of a decision, but if allowing others to make it could strengthen their leadership, you may want to skip the meeting. While you could attend your friend's open house, they might not have a strong interest in whether you are there or not. Taking the evening off to rest could be a wiser choice. Remember that in either case, your focus should be on others. Within the limits of your own energy and resources, ask, "How can I help others by being present?" and "Will my absence be positive, negative, or neutral in its effect on others?"

Presentation and Demeanor

I once led a small group in which two of the attendees exerted an equally strong—and opposite—influence by their presence. One man—I'll call him Jake—was usually a few minutes late for our meetings. He generally came straight from work at a small business he owned, and he often seemed a bit harried and wore a pained expression. Whatever he'd experienced that day stuck to his face like glue, and his demeanor was stressed and anxious. Jake was about six foot two, and as our meeting progressed he would frequently sit forward a bit with his head hung low until someone would venture to ask, "Jake, what's up? You seem a little off tonight." With that prompting, Jake would unburden his mind about a run-in with a vendor, a near miss he'd had in traffic, or a long list of the problems his industry was facing.

The other man—I'll call him Robert—was a retired fellow and a widower. Though he lived on a fixed income, he always managed to dress well. Generally, Robert arrived a few minutes ahead of our group meeting and helped me set up chairs. He often stayed a few minutes afterward as well, chatting with the other attendees. Robert was no more than five foot six, yet he sat comfortably erect with one leg casually crossed over the other. He was a quiet man, and never the first to speak when a discussion started. When Robert did offer an opinion, it was in a calm tone that aimed to bring consensus.

Both men vividly illustrate the next aspect of presence, which is personal presentation and demeanor. By arriving late, wearing disheveled work clothes, and communicating through his facial expression and posture that something was amiss, Jake often derailed our meetings just as they were getting started. He generally swung the group in a negative direction even before saying a word. Robert, on the other hand, managed to exert a positive influence on the group simply by being in the room. His dress, demeanor, and comportment were appropriate and inviting, and he always set a positive tone.

Because your presence is basically you and everything about you, all aspects of your personal presentation can affect your influence in this area. Here are a few things to pay special attention to as you consider the way your presence works on others.

Dress

Everyone has a personal style, whether it's cool and casual, dressed and pressed, or a little bit of grunge. The way you dress reveals something about you, and no one style is inherently better than another. Your style does communicate something, however, and it's important to remember that not all modes of dress are appropriate for all occasions. Attending a formal reception in shorts and flip-flops will certainly communicate that you are comfortable and approachable, but it may also communicate a lack of respect for the guest of honor. Wearing casual dress slacks and loafers to a beach party may show that you are a tidy, orderly person, but it may also indicate that you have little interest in participating in the event.

With a few exceptions (for example, when black tie is requested, or where there is an office dress code), there are no firm rules about how we dress. Just keep in mind that the way you present yourself in terms of clothing and hygiene is part of your overall presence. Be yourself, of course, but think about others as well, and how your appearance will affect your interactions with them.

COMPORTMENT

Comportment is your manner of bearing, such as your demeanor, posture, facial expressions, and so forth. It is how you look and the vibe you give off to those around you. It's easy to tell when someone, like Jake in my small group, is out of sorts. You can see it in their facial expression, their slouch, the listless way in which they walk, and in semi-verbal clues such as sighs or yawns. The act of walking into a room initiates your presence. The way you comport yourself establishes what that presence will be.

Remember that your presence—in fact, every aspect of your influence—is an inherently social phenomenon. You are present *with others*. Things like appearing sullen, slouching, resting your head in your hands, and staring out the window may come naturally to you, but they may also communicate to others "You don't matter," or "I'd rather be somewhere else."

Be fully present wherever you choose to be. It is your choice, after all. Take responsibility for that choice by presenting yourself in a pleasant and appropriate way. Smile. Be attentive. Remain alert. Focus your attention on others or the matter at hand. Communicate through your facial expression, posture, and attentiveness that you are engaged with the people you've chosen to spend time with.

Manners

Manners are generally accepted rules for polite social behavior. These are things like remaining silent while others are speaking and silencing your cell phone in a movie theater. Like many other aspects of presence, your manners are invisible to you but plain as day to everyone else. Our culture prizes individualism to such a degree that the very concept of manners may seem obsolete. However, when a client insists on checking social media accounts during your presentation, or a neighbor plays loud music late at night, you quickly realize that the subtle ways we show either respect or contempt for others really do matter.

To create a positive presence, give attention to these casual, habitual actions that can either make or break your influence:

- Stand when someone enters the room.
- When you are a guest, remain standing until invited to sit.
- Greet people when introduced, and introduce others.
- Make eye contact with the person to whom you are speaking.
- Avoid taking calls or checking messages on your phone during meetings or conversations.
- Say "thank you" when offered anything, even if you decline the offer.
- Invite others to be served ahead of yourself.
- Greet everyone you meet with a smile.
- Avoid gratuitous criticism of others.
- Don't repeat unflattering things about another person, even if they're true.
- Don't tailgate.
- Be on time.
- When entering a building, hold the door open for the next person.

- Don't talk with food in your mouth.

- Silence your cell phone in public places.

- Discipline your own children diligently and other people's children not at all.

- Speak pleasantly to waiters and clerks, even when they make mistakes.

- Don't use foul language in public.

- Don't offer your opinion unless asked.

- Say little about your own achievements.

- Don't talk too much.

Displaying good manners really boils down to treating others as you would like to be treated.[5] Do that, and your presence will likely be sweet and welcome. Your influence will surely grow.

Online Persona

We have been speaking of presence in terms of in-person contact with others—and for many of us, that's the primary way we leave our footprints on the world. However, through social media accounts, blogs, comments, and of course emails, each of us also creates an online presence that has the same potential to enhance or degrade our influence. We are present with people in a virtual realm every day, and those interactions can be even more powerful and long lasting than those created through our physical presence.

Also, we may create an online persona, perhaps unintentionally, that is very different from our physical presence. This happens for two reasons.

1. We filter our online image by carefully selecting the items we post, especially photos, to make us appear in the best possible light.

To read some people's social media feeds, you might think they were the happiest, wealthiest, thinnest, most exciting folk who ever lived! Their online interactions show only the most positive aspects of their lives, and only the most flattering angles of themselves.

Without intending to, we can create an inflated or unrealistically positive persona in the online sphere. That kind of presence can actually undermine your influence by making you seem false or unapproachable. Everybody has problems, after all.

2. WE DON'T ALWAYS FILTER THE THINGS WE SAY TO OR ABOUT OTHERS ONLINE.

The distance and quasi anonymity of the internet make it all too easy to say things online that we would likely never say in real life. We may be more direct, more prone to insult someone or express outrage, and more liable to repeat questionable information than we would be among a group of neighbors or friends. Without meaning to, we can create an online presence that is cynical, angry, judgmental, or just plain negative.

Treat your online presence in the same way you do your in-person existence. Realize that you do have a presence in the digital world, examine whether it is positive or negative, and take steps to project a winsome nature to those you meet online. Be present in the places where your presence is welcome and expected. Remain absent in the places where your presence might be detrimental to others. Without being false or hypocritical, let your demeanor communicate warmth through positive interactions, compliments, and helpful comments. Remember that humor doesn't always come across as well online as it does in person. Be careful when making jokes lest they be taken as insults. Be polite. Use good manners.

Your digital footprint can magnify your actual presence and extend it to places you could never otherwise go. That offers tremendous potential for extending your influence. It also carries with it the danger of easily damaging your influence through carelessness. Let your online image match your physical presence in warmth and positivity, and your influence will grow accordingly.

FOR OTHERS

Simply by being who you are, right where you are, you can have an impact on others. Being present with them and just being your-self offers a gift of respect and dignity. That's just as true in a corporate boardroom as it is in a refugee camp. People are blessed by your inten-tional presence, which disposes them to respect you and accept your influence in their lives.

It's important to remember, however, that the act of presence must be done for others, not for ourselves. We must be self-aware in order to be intentionally present, but we must also set aside our needs in order to focus on others.

Author Barry Corey observed this principle in action one day in Fullerton, California. Corey was going for a run in the city when he noticed two men ahead of him on the sidewalk. Based on their appea-ranace, Corey judged them to be homeless men and quickly jogged around them. One of the men had, in his hand, a bag from a fast-food eatery.

Just then, the taller man called out, "Hey, Barry."

Corey turned around to see a man he knew, a university professor who was a national expert in his field.

"What are you doing here at this time of day?" Corey asked. The professor tried to avoid answering directly, but Barry pressed for a response. Finally, the latter came clean.

"My friend and I every so often go to McDonald's early in the morning and buy a bag of Egg McMuffins. Then we walk around the city streets to find drifters, and we have breakfast with them."[6]

How incredible that a man of this stature would get up early to sim-ply spend time sharing a meal with homeless people. This man's pres-ence affected the life of at least one homeless man, and his example has influenced countless others—including you and me.

This is the power of presence, and that power is available to you every day. It simply involves being with others for their benefit and not yours. Though you should not offer your presence in the hope of a reward, when you invest yourself in others, that gift is returned in intangible ways. It is an investment in the future.

●●●●●●●●●●●●●●●●●●● **THE KEY THREE** ●●●●●●●●●●●●●●●●●●●

1. Consider your presence both in person and online. Determine whether it is currently positive or negative.

2. Name two key areas mentioned in this chapter in which you might improve your presence.

3. Name one person or group of people with whom you will be intentionally present this week.

THE POWER OF YOUR ENCOURAGEMENT

When you're kind to others, you help yourself;
when you're cruel to others you hurt yourself.

PROVERBS 11:17 (MSG)

A young woman I'll call Helen was teaching math to junior-high students, which is never an easy task. By the end of the week, the students were feeling the stress of learning a new concept. Their nerves were frayed, and their faces showed frustration. Some were becoming snarky with one another and with Helen.

Realizing that the class would spiral into negativity without some intervention, the young teacher arrived at an idea. She asked the students to take a sheet of paper and write the name of each person in the class. "I told them to think of the nicest thing they could say about each of their classmates and write it down," said Helen. Students took the rest of the hour to finish the assignment, then turned in their papers. "They seemed more relaxed," she observed.

Over the weekend, Helen wrote the name of each student on a sheet of paper and listed the positive comments the other students had made about him or her. The following week, she gave each student their list. Within moments, smiles broke out around the room.

"Really?" one student whispered. "I never knew that meant anything to anyone."

"I didn't know anyone liked me that much!" another student exclaimed.

Helen was satisfied that the assignment had accomplished its purpose by raising everyone's spirits, and she never mentioned it again.

A number of years later, Helen attended the funeral of one of those students, a bright young man who was killed while serving his country in wartime. The church was packed with the friends of this young man, "Mark," including many former classmates. Afterward, Helen attended a gathering at Mark's parents' home, along with many of her former students. Mark's parents approached Helen and said, "We want to show you something. Mark was carrying this when he was killed." With that, his father produced a paper from a wallet. It was the list of what Mark's classmates had written about him.

"Thank you so much for doing that," Mark's mother said. "As you can see, Mark treasured it."

Some of the former classmates overheard. One said, "I still have my list. It's in my top desk drawer at home." Another said, "I have mine, too. It's in my diary." "I put mine in our wedding album," said another. "I bet we all saved them," a fourth student chimed in. "I carry mine with me at all times."

"That's when I finally sat down and cried," Helen says. "The lesson my former students taught me that day became a standard in every class I taught for the rest of my teaching career."[1]

This story illustrates two basic truths about encouragement: The first is that everyone needs it—craves it, in fact—and treasures it. The second is that you may never realize the tremendous power your encouraging words will have on another human soul. When you encourage others, you unleash a positive power that will far outlive the few moments it takes to speak the words. Your encouragement can change a person's life forever.

Encouragement is a particular form of positive speech that takes your influence to a new level. When you encourage others, you directly affect their thoughts about themselves, their situation, and their future. The results can be astounding. In this chapter, you will discover the explosive power of encouragement and be motivated to practice it consistently in all your relationships.

HOW ENCOURAGEMENT WORKS

Encouragement is hopeful affirmation offered to another person, particularly when they have experienced some form of disappointment, failure, or loss. Encouragement dwells in the middle space between compliments and constructive advice. Without minimizing the reality of one's current situation, it inspires hope for the future.

When someone misses a promotion at work or is denied entry into their preferred university, they will be disappointed. Indeed, they may realize something painful about themselves because of that frustrating experience. However, encouragement does not dwell on that reality but points to a better future: "You'll bounce back from this. I see how determined you are, and I know you're going to succeed."

When a person goes through a divorce, their feelings of rejection, disappointment, or shame may be acute. A word of encouragement helps lift their sights beyond that. "Many people love you, and you are not alone." "You're a strong, confident person, and I know you will get through this."

When you encourage another, you demonstrate sincerity and empathy. When others see that you understand their pain and genuinely care about them, you gain influence in their lives. But please note that this should never be done with the ulterior motive of gaining influence. Encouragement, like a compliment, must be given for another's benefit. We encourage others only because we truly sympathize with their need.

What Encouragement Is Not

When offering encouragement, it may be tempting to reach for any positive statement in an attempt to lift another's spirits. That's dangerous because even those who are emotionally low have a keen sense of reality. They know when they're being offered platitudes or unrealistically optimistic statements. When encouraging others, you must beware of offering the following three types of false encouragement.

Flattery

Flattery is excessive or insincere praise, especially when given for the benefit of the speaker rather than the hearer. When the boss fails to deliver on a big project, it may be tempting to say, "You're still the best boss I've ever had. This company is lucky to have you!" Some of that may be true, but it will ring false if the boss realizes you're only buttering her up in order to gain a promotion, or you're trying to minimize your part in the failure. Don't offer encouragement you don't stand behind. People long to be shown the silver lining in a bad situation, but they resent flattery or condescension.

DENIAL OF REALITY

Encouragement is not a denial of the facts, no matter how bleak they may be. On the contrary, it is an offer of affirmation or hope within the negative circumstance. Telling someone, "Don't worry, it'll all work out," after their mother has been given a terminal diagnosis is not sound encouragement. It's better to offer an encouraging statement that deals fully with the facts at hand: "I'll be with you, and we'll get through this together." When in doubt, it is better to say nothing than to appear unconcerned or out of touch with the reality another person faces.

FALSE PROMISES

An offer of help can be a great way to encourage others. It lets them know they're not alone and provides some hope for a solution. However, a false promise can do more harm than good. When a friend has a legal problem, it may be tempting to say, "We'll get to the bottom of this. Justice will be done." Unless you're a lawyer, that's likely a promise you can't keep. And even attorneys avoid promising to control the result of a legal proceeding. You can offer to seek justice, but you can't promise a particular outcome. You can promise to help someone financially, but beware of promising to resolve a person's debts. You can offer help to a sick friend, but you can't promise they'll get well. Desperate people latch on to hope wherever they can find it. Don't make an unwise promise that will lead to further disappointment.

Why Encouragement Matters

When you've just enjoyed a satisfying meal, it can be difficult to imagine what hunger is like. In the same way, when your circumstances are good, it can be hard to understand why encouragement has such power in a person's life. But encouragement matters for at least three reasons.

LIFE IS HARD

Life is difficult, and that's true even when there is no obvious crisis in a person's life. We never know the burdens and trials another person may be facing. A popular saying widely misattributed to Plato states, "Be kind, for everyone you meet is fighting a hard battle." As if to prove the veracity of that statement, it was likely written by a man named John Watson (a real person, though, not Sherlock Holmes's friend). A version of the quote appeared in *The British Weekly* in 1897.[2] Perhaps one of Watson's burdens may have been that other people got the credit for his work. How frustrating! Others carry more profound inner burdens, such as the loss of a child, a chronic illness, an unloving spouse, or the pain of an embarrassing failure. Though they may never reveal that struggle, it can remain with them every day, even for a lifetime. That means nearly every person you meet could benefit from a word of encouragement, regardless of how cheerful they may appear. When you make yourself an encourager, you become a welcome and sought-after presence in others' lives.

EVERYONE NEEDS AFFIRMATION

Encouragement is vital because all human beings want and need affirmation. Sure, there are a few folks who act as if they don't care what others think. And there may even be a tiny minority who are truly unconcerned about the opinions of others. But the vast majority of human beings long to be noticed, valued, and affirmed. Even people with a normal level of self-esteem enjoy—and occasionally need—words of affirmation. When you encourage others, you take on a wonderful, positive role in their lives. Genuine encouragers are much loved and highly respected. They become great influencers.

DISCOURAGERS ABOUND

Discouragement is a far more common experience than is encouragement. For every positive voice that offers hope, comfort, and affirmation, a person is likely to encounter ten voices that express annoyance, doubt, or frustration. Even if you have a high level of self-esteem, a steady barrage of discouraging talk is bound to affect your spirits. We all need a few positive voices to counterbalance the negative ones we hear throughout the day. Encouragement is like a gentle breeze. You never know exactly when to expect it, but it's refreshing whenever it comes.

Encouragement really works. It produces a marvelous, often instantaneous, positive effect on others. Dale Carnegie observed,

> Tell your child, your spouse, or your employee that he or she is stupid or dumb at a certain thing, has no gift for it, and is doing it all wrong, and you have destroyed almost every incentive to try to improve. But use the opposite technique—be liberal with your encouragement...let the other person know that you have faith in his ability to do it...and he will practice until the dawn comes in at the window in order to excel.[3]

Everyone needs encouragement. When you provide genuine words of affirmation and appreciation, you open a window of hope into a weary soul. You exercise influence of the noblest type, that which is born of deep concern for others.

HOW TO BE AN ENCOURAGER

Now that you understand what encouragement is and isn't, let's talk about how to become an encourager. For some, this comes naturally. You may be the type of person who is always attuned to the needs of others and liberal with words of affirmation. If so, that's great. These ideas will add to your repertoire of encouragement. Others are less naturally inclined to offer encouragement. They may be less likely to notice when others need affirmation, or have a harder time finding words that offer authentic encouragement rather than false hope. If that describes you, this section will show you when and how to encourage others. Let's begin by learning the occasions when encouragement may be most needed.

When to Encourage

The first obstacle some people face in becoming an encourager is knowing when to offer a word of affirmation or reassurance. Nobody wants to come off as a false encourager, constantly offering pick-me-ups that are unneeded and perhaps unwelcome. The good news is that, other than during an acute crisis, there really is no wrong time to offer encouragement. When someone has just received a diagnosis or is grieving a recent loss, sharing sorrows may be more welcome than words of cheer. People need some time to absorb the shock of their circumstances and to mourn loss. However, at virtually any other time, encouragement will be welcome. Be especially alert for the following opportunities to encourage others.

When They're Struggling

Encourage others whenever you notice they are struggling in life, with health, or in their work, schooling, relationships, finances, or career—to list a few examples. Some of these occasions are obvious and difficult not to notice. When a person experiences a serious illness, injury, divorce, or loss of a loved one, everyone around them is likely to know about it. But remember that many struggles exist below the surface. How are you to know when someone is facing a significant problem in life? More often than not, they'll tell you.

Watch your social media feed, and you'll see lots of people sharing their need for encouragement. They'll mention a problem in their family, an illness, difficulties in their relationships, loneliness, and even boredom. Some of these cries for encouragement may be voiced as complaints, but look deeper. And when you engage in conversation with people at work, school, or church, you'll often hear direct statements of their need, though you may pass over them lightly. When others request prayer, express frustration, voice a fear, or even grumble, they're giving clues to the burdens they carry. Don't miss those calls for encouragement.

When They're Working Hard

The next time you're at a restaurant, take a moment to observe your server—not just when they're at your table, but as they go about their work. You'll likely see a person who is extremely busy, in almost constant motion, and working hard. Are they unhappy? Probably not. They may love their work and be energized by the dinnertime rush. But expending all that energy is likely to take a toll. Try saying, "Wow, you're working hard and doing a great job," and see how their face brightens. Anyone engaged in a difficult task is a candidate for encouragement, even though they may appear to have everything under control.

Be aware of the effort that others expend in other contexts as well. Notice the energy your spouse puts in to earning a living, parenting, and maintaining your home. See the effort it takes for your children to complete homework, athletic training, or music practice. Observe the concentration and focus of a coworker who is pushing hard to meet a project deadline. Any of them may be like a waiter at a restaurant— not unhappy, but becoming tired, grateful to be affirmed for their hard work. Encourage those who are working hard in any pursuit.

When They Fail

Failure is not unlike the other kinds of struggles mentioned earlier, but it carries an added feature. Those who fail experience not only a sense of loss, but also a sense of shame or responsibility. That can be true in a business failure, the failure of a project, the loss of a game, a divorce, a bankruptcy, and in countless other situations when the result is not the one hoped for. The sense of personal embarrassment or shame heightens the need for encouragement in the wake of a failure. To make matters worse, a person's pride may hinder them from seeking the community and camaraderie in which encouragement naturally flows. Be alert to those around you who have experienced failure. They are ripe for encouragement.

Whenever

Remember what we learned earlier in this chapter: everyone you meet is facing a hard battle, though you may not be aware of it. Though they may show no signs, most people have a deep inner struggle, burden, or need that causes them to welcome and even crave the affirmation of others. Don't wait until you discover a specific need. Be an all-purpose encourager. Be willing to affirm others in any and every situation.

Types of Encouragement

"But I don't know what to say." That may be the most common objection to offering encouragement. Some folk are not apt with words, and they struggle to know what to say to someone who has been through a divorce, lost a loved one, or is facing a personal crisis. Realizing that flattery and false hope are unwelcome, they fear saying anything at all. When you are stuck for words, consider offering encouragement in one of these categories.

PERSONAL AFFIRMATION

You may not know what to say about a situation, and you certainly can't make predictions about the future. But you can always say something kind about the individual. "I really like you." "You're a good person." "You've been a good daughter." "You have done well." If offered sincerely, any positive statement about another person will be both welcome and encouraging. Everyone wants and needs to be appreciated, regardless of the situation they face. This may be the simplest and easiest type of encouragement to offer because every person has value, and each person can be affirmed for the good within them.

ACKNOWLEDGMENT OF EFFORT

When I was young, my baseball coach Frank Ramsey understood the power of encouragement as a motivator. While some coaches yelled loudly and berated their players for mistakes, he always found something positive to affirm in a player, even when giving correction. "Great swing! Just remember to keep your feet planted." "You've got a great arm; now we have to work on your control." "Good hustle! We'll get 'em next time." Being acknowledged for what they did right made the players more willing to hear correction and more eager to try again.

When someone has tried and failed, affirm the effort. You're not giving absolution or ignoring their shortcomings. You're simply acknowledging the sweat and struggle they expended. You're pointing to the good they did rather than dwelling on what they failed to do.

WORDS OF HOPE

Hope is what any discouraged person longs for. They're desperate to know if things will be okay and if they have a future. You may not have the answer to their specific questions, but you can offer hope based on eternal truths. The sun actually will come up tomorrow. The world will continue to turn, the seasons will change, and life will go on. Simply being reminded of this can bring hope in the face of disappointment. And in some cases, you may be able to offer even more particular hope based on your knowledge of the situation. While you must avoid minimizing the loss or frustration that a person is experiencing, you can still offer words of hope like these:

- "You're a young person, and I believe you can bounce back from this."
- "In a year from now, your life may be in a very different place."
- "People won't remember your failure so much as that you tried your best."
- "Tomorrow is another day, and we can try again."

Encouragement always looks to the future. Words of hope are encouragement in one of its most powerful forms.

PRESENCE

There are times when words are hard to come by and unnecessary. Your presence at key times in life is an encouragement all by itself. Visiting a hospital, attending a funeral, stopping by after work, hanging out on a Saturday—each of these gestures may be an encouragement to others regardless of the words exchanged, if any at all.

Ways to Encourage

Just as there are several types of encouragement, and each may fit slightly better in one situation than another, there are also various ways to offer encouragement. The first way we generally think of is through words of affirmation. We say something encouraging to others. Yet there are other ways, including nonverbal ways, to encourage a person. And even when we use words, there are a variety of ways to deliver them. Let's think about some of the ways in which we might encourage another person.

Casual Comments

Encouragement often takes the form of words, but those words need not be formal or rehearsed. In fact, the more purposeful we are in crafting words of encouragement, the harder it may be to deliver them with sincerity and authenticity. The most welcome words of encouragement are often delivered off the cuff: "Great job!" "Nice try." "I'm praying for you." Don't wait for a formal occasion to encourage a friend. You can do this in the moment. Offer encouragement right on the spot, as soon as you notice the opportunity. As long as your words are sincere, they need not be well rehearsed.

Public Praise

Few things are more encouraging than to be singled out in a positive away among family, friends, or peers. When you have the opportunity to encourage someone in front of others, that praise or affirmation will carry double the weight. When a coworker returns to work after an illness, you can publicly welcome her, say how much she has been missed, and express hope for the team's success with her back on the job. When your team has lost a contest, it will hearten each of the players to hear their valiant effort affirmed out loud.

While encouragement regarding sensitive matters must be delivered privately, personal affirmation and acknowledgment of effort can often be delivered in public. Correct privately, praise publicly. Remember that rule, and your words of affirmation will always be welcome.

Handwritten Notes

A casual word is always helpful, but a handwritten note can become a valued keepsake, delivering encouragement for days or even years to come. Several years ago a woman wrote to an advice columnist to express her appreciation for those who sent notes of encouragement when she faced a devastating life crisis. She said, "When I began to receive notes of comfort and encouragement, I discovered how remarkable the healing power of true friendship can be. Please tell your readers that any show of concern will help. The simple sentence, 'I'm sorry about your trouble,' says it all."

The columnist agreed. She responded, "Many people are inclined not to say anything for fear they will cause embarrassment or open old wounds. Wrong. A word of compassion and encouragement is always appreciated."[4] And when that word of encouragement is written by hand, it may be even more appreciated because of the extra effort required to deliver it.

ELECTRONIC COMMUNICATION

Electronic media has the tremendous value of immediacy. They make it possible to deliver instant encouragement to nearly anyone within seconds of discovering the need. A text, email, or social media message that says, "Thinking of you" can cut through a person's loneliness and offer hope.

Just remember that the ease of such communications may make them prone to overuse. As with all forms of encouragement, e-messages must be authentic and heartfelt in order to be welcome and effective. Also, because they are so quick and easy to deliver, e-messages may carry less weight than an in-person visit, phone call, or handwritten note. By all means, use electronic communications. But be aware that other channels of affirmation may be needed as well.

GIFTS

Gifts can be a form of encouragement that is especially useful for those who have difficulty putting their thoughts into words, or on occasions when more overt communications might be intrusive. Interestingly, the act of giving a gift is the real encouragement, more so than the gift itself. Flowers will last only a few days, but the act of sending them delivers a cheerful message that will be long remembered. It says, "I'm thinking of you." A gift of food wordlessly communicates, "I'm here to help." Beyond the words printed on a greeting card, the gift's arrival in the mail will say, "You are important to me." These messages are deeply encouraging and a pleasure to receive.

NONVERBAL AFFIRMATION

There are many other nonverbal ways to encourage another, such as hugs, pats on the back, nods, smiles, high fives, or thumbs-up gestures. These casual signals offer affirmation or demonstrate concern without a word spoken. Remember that any form of touch, such as a hug, requires a good deal of tact and sensitivity in order for it to be welcome and meaningful. When you are alert for them, you'll find opportunities to deliver a smile or high five many times a day. These are great modes of encouragement for "whenever."

YOUR CHOICE

We each face a choice when it comes to encouraging others. We can be alert to the needs of others, sensitive to their hurts and struggles, and willing to offer support for the challenges they face. Or we can insulate ourselves from their concerns, focusing on our narrow channel of interaction with them as a coworker, neighbor, or classmate, while ignoring their deeper needs. That's the easier choice in some ways. It allows us to maintain a comfortable distance from the sometimes-messy and troubling struggles others face.

Yet when you make the choice to be an encourager, you'll find that something remarkable happens. You gain a network of friends and acquaintances with whom you share life. You receive encouragement as well as give it. You develop relationships that go beyond the surface concerns of chatting about the weather or cooperating on a project. You make friends.

In the end, the choice you make about encouraging others is really a choice about your own character and the type of life you'll lead. Will you close yourself to others, holding them at an emotional arm's length? Or will you dive into life with them, sharing their joys and sorrows, triumphs and failures? Will you be an encourager?

For those who are eager to extend their influence and affect the world in positive ways, that's an easy choice to make.

THE KEY THREE

1. Consider this question: *Does encouraging others come naturally to me?* If so, why? And if not, why not?

2. Review the types of encouragement and ways to deliver encouragement listed in this chapter. Identify those you think you can most readily use.

3. List three people you know who may be in need of encouragement, and encourage them before the end of the day.

THE POWER OF
YOUR GENEROSITY

Gain all you can. Save all you can. Give all you can.

JOHN WESLEY[1]

In 1976 a young man named Tom graduated with honors from Claremont McKenna College in California and accepted a position in his family's business back home in Kansas City. Tom worked hard and was soon promoted. In 1981, after automating the company's office network, he was elected president of a division. Later, he coordinated efforts with the US government to create an innovative plan that allowed online access for millions of Americans who deal with the federal government each year, eliminating millions of pages of paperwork. Tom was promoted to president of the entire company in 1989 and named CEO in 1992.[2]

Despite Tom's success in the business world—and the million-dollar annual income that went with it—he felt that something was missing from his life. After a good deal of soul searching, Tom Bloch made an astounding decision. He resigned as CEO of H&R Block, the world's largest tax preparation firm, to take a job teaching math to middle schoolers at St. Francis Xavier, an inner-city parochial school.

You might think the decision to generously give his time and talent to educate young people would have satisfied Tom's need for "more," but his generosity was just getting started. One night while browsing the internet, he noticed that the youth volunteer participation rate in Kansas City was very low. After sharing his concern with his wife,

Mary, the Blochs took action and founded the Youth Service Alliance of Greater Kansas City. That effort is one of several causes the couple has supported through the Thomas M. and Mary S. Bloch Philanthropic Fund.[3] Tom later cofounded University Academy, a public charter school in Kansas City. The school has grown to more than one thousand students, and over the last five years all but two graduates have gone on to attend college, an amazing success rate for an urban school.[4]

Tom's story illustrates the incredible power of generosity to change the world around you. When you give voluntarily to others and without obligation, you unleash a power that can transform their lives—and yours too. In this chapter, you will discover why generosity is such an effective form of influence and a potent agent for change. Like Tom Bloch, you may discover the greater purpose you've been missing in your own life.

GENEROSITY AND INFLUENCE

Generosity is giving to others without expectation or obligation. You can be generous with time, abilities, resources, and in many other ways, but the key element in each case is giving without an expectation of return. When you hope to receive something back after giving to someone, whether it's interest on a loan or even a favor in return, you're not being generous—you're making an investment. Generosity is a pure contribution. It's a donation made to charity, with or without a tax deduction. It's a favor offered to someone who cannot possibly return it. It's sharing ideas or sales leads or business contacts with someone who needs them, knowing that those assets may be lost to you. Generosity is a gift, plain and simple, and it influences others in three ways.

1. Generosity is leadership by example.

Your generosity shows others what is most important to you. When you put your time, energy, money, or other resources into something, your contribution puts a neon sign over that need to say, "This matters!" You draw attention to your highest priorities by generously providing your time, talent, and treasure to them.

2. Generosity has a nudge effect, prompting others to be generous also.

You may have noticed that when one person volunteers for a task, others are more likely to join in. The first volunteer helps others overcome their internal resistance. When you share anything, from money to ideas to space at the table, you'll prompt others to join you.

3. Generosity builds trust.

When your giving is truly generous, it is done without expectation—a pure sacrifice. As we'll see in a later chapter, sacrifice on the part of a leader is a powerful motivator. When others realize that you are more concerned for their needs—or for the poor, the marginalized, or others who are struggling—than you are for yourself, they will be far more likely to trust your leadership or advice.

Generosity should never be practiced in the hope of reward, yet we can easily recognize the correlation between liberal giving and respect. When you give of yourself, you influence others. When you withhold your resources from others, your influence will diminish. Generosity commands attention.

SCARCITY VERSUS ABUNDANCE

Generosity does not come easily to everyone. We are all wired to put ourselves first, so the thought of giving away resources, especially money, sets off alarm bells in our subconscious. *How do I know the need is legitimate? What if people take advantage of me? What happens when I run short of money, time, or ideas?*

These questions are quite natural. For one thing, we're trained to be responsible for ourselves, so we believe that we should look after our own needs, and everyone else should do the same. We figure that the world works only if each person pulls their own weight.

Also, most people have at least a little natural suspicion of others. In some of us, that wariness is more acute, to the point that we find it hard to trust people who present themselves as being in need. "What are they hiding?" we may wonder. "Maybe it's their own fault they're in this situation." We can also be skeptical about the results of generosity.

People have been giving to the poor for thousands of years, yet poverty still exists. What difference does our generosity really make?

Finally, we're all just a little bit selfish at heart. We realize that there will be only one certain result of giving our money away: we won't have it anymore!

Nearly all of our objections to generosity can be traced to a single idea. This thought runs like an electric current through all our hesitations to be charitable. It causes us to cling tightly to the things we have and resist sharing with others. This idea is called *scarcity thinking*.

Scarcity thinking is based on the notion that all resources are both finite and in short supply. In this mind-set, everything that exists has a firm limit, and once exhausted it can never be replenished. For example, if I have two dollars and I give one to you, I have become poorer. Money is scarce, and I don't know how I will ever replace the dollar I gave away. If I share my ideas with you, you'll succeed and I won't because good ideas are rare and hard to find. If I volunteer my time for a charitable organization, I'll have less time to do the things that matter to me because there are only 24 hours in a day. That's a snapshot of scarcity thinking.

When we believe that everything we possess is in short supply, we'll resist sharing them with others and possibly never even use them ourselves. Scarcity thinking causes us to withdraw from others and hoard what we have.

But there is another way to look at the world, and it is the polar opposite of scarcity thinking. It's called an *abundance mind-set*. Abundance thinking is based on the belief that nearly everything is plentiful or at least renewable, so there is always more where it came from. While it is true that many things have a firm limit—the hours in a day, for example, or the square footage of a piece of real estate—value is unlimited. We create more of it every day. There is no limit to the number of good ideas your mind can produce. You always have the possibility of earning more money. More food can be grown, more clothing bought, more friends made, and more wealth created. People who think this way are never afraid of running out because they know the things that matter most in life are truly unlimited. Relationships, ideas, friendship, cooperation, contentment, opportunity, and love have no finite boundary.

You may be thinking, "But they're wrong! My wallet has only twenty dollars in it, and when it's gone, it's gone." On one level, of course, you're right. It is possible to run out of money or food or time. Yet abundance thinkers have discovered that a lifestyle of generosity not only provides for their needs, but actually produces better results than does scarcity thinking. Rather than running short of resources, abundance thinkers continually find themselves encountering more. Those who practice generosity find that they receive it in return.

This idea is nothing new. It's confirmed by the wisdom of the Bible, for Jesus said, "Give, and it will be given to you. A good measure, pressed down, shaken together and running over, will be poured into your lap. For with the measure you use, it will be measured to you."[5] The contemporary saying, "What goes around, comes around," expresses a similar idea. Whatever you put forth into the world, you will eventually receive in return. When you are generous, others will be generous with you. When you share ideas, more good ideas will come to you. When you welcome a new person into your circle of friends, you don't lose your place, you gain a new friend. When you share time, money, encouragement, ideas, or resources of any kind, you'll find yourself encountering more of the same—maybe not immediately, but sometime soon. Openhanded people eventually discover that the world opens its hand to them in return.

The opposite is true as well. Scarcity thinking produces scarcity. When you close yourself to others, they close themselves to you. When you hoard your resources, others don't benefit from them, and you may not either. When you refuse to share ideas, you cut yourself off from discussions, contacts, and opportunities. When you offer a closed fist to the world, you're likely to receive bare knuckles in return.

When you give generously, you change the world and yourself in important ways. You meet a need in others, which is always a hopeful and positive thing to do. By sharing, you begin to create your vision for the future.

Generosity also meets a need within you. Like Tom Bloch, you too have a desire for "more" in your life. You want your life to count for something. You may be trying to succeed in your career, master your craft, or even make a lot of money, but deep down you hunger for something more significant. You want meaning, purpose, and value in your life. When you make the choice to be generous, you will discover that purpose. You'll find that when you volunteer your time for others, you don't have less time for yourself; instead, you enjoy your time all the more. When you give money to others, you find greater satisfaction in meeting their needs than in spending on yourself. When you practice hospitality, you don't lose your privacy but gain valued relationships. Generosity is a golden key that unlocks the true treasures of the universe: friendship, purpose, and fulfillment.

HOW TO BE GENEROUS

When you hear the word *generosity*, you probably think first about money. The term is often used by those asking for a financial contribution. We receive those pitches all the time, pleas to contribute money to a charity, a religious organization, a radio station, or even a panhandler on the street. Indeed, financial giving is the first and most obvious way of practicing generosity, but it is by no means the only one. Think holistically about generosity, and you will quickly realize there are many ways to be generous. We will begin our discussion with finances, but we'll go on to explore seven other ways to be generous toward others.

Donating Money

Donating money is a primary way to practice generosity because money fills such a variety of needs. It can provide food, shelter, clothing, medical care, labor, or just about any tangible thing. Once you have adopted an abundance mind-set, giving money away is much less intimidating, especially when you are convinced of the need. And giving is even easier to do when you make it part of your financial plan.

Many people designate charitable giving in their budget. Some follow the time-honored practice of the *tithe,* setting aside ten percent of their income for donation to their faith community or other worthy causes. While that may seem like a lot, there are many folks who give even more, offering sizable gifts to worthy causes even beyond their budgeted amount. Remarkably, this practice seems to make the remaining dollars stretch even further, as purposeful giving requires careful budgeting.

Some wonder about the result of their giving, refusing to donate to any cause unless they are convinced the money is being used ethically and is producing tangible results. It is certainly wise to be sure that any organization you contribute to is reputable and well managed, and it is sometimes appropriate to designate the purpose of a donation. But beware of trying to micromanage the use of your contributions. A donation is a gift. When you give it, you surrender control of the funds.

Others wonder about the wisdom of on-the-spot generosity, such as contributions made to an organization soliciting funds outside a shopping center, or handouts given to a person on the street. What if the money is misused? What if a panhandler uses it to buy alcohol or drugs? There is no one-size-fits-all methodology for handling such opportunities. You must let your conscience be your guide. And remember that one of the joys of giving is responding to urgent needs that touch your heart. When you feel prompted to give, do so. Certainly, you'll want to give funds wisely. But don't allow fear or suspicion to prevent you from doing good.

Spending Time

Your presence is a gift, and spending your time with others or on their behalf is a way of being generous. Time is the most precious resource we have because it represents our very lives. We may not like to think of it, but our days really are numbered. When you spend your time, you are parting with a portion of your life. And time really is money for a great number of people. Anyone whose income is tied to productivity realizes the dollar value of an hour. At the time of this writing, it's currently worth $7.25. For many artists and professionals, an hour of time is worth far more than that.

Spending your time is a gift—and when you think of it that way, it is actually more inviting to be generous in this area. Let's put a nominal value on your time. For the sake of this discussion, we'll say that an hour is worth 20 dollars. So if you volunteer three hours a week to teach literacy, you're not only helping someone learn to read but also contributing perhaps 60 dollars per week to a good cause, including the value of your preparation time and commuting. Over the course of a year, you could easily add more than $3,000 of value to a wonderful organization.

In practice, of course, it costs you less than that to be generous with your time. When you spend 15 minutes on the phone offering wisdom to a friend, you've given a gift that may produce incalculable results. When you spend the afternoon at a wedding, or stay after work to lend a hand to a coworker, or babysit for an evening so a single mom can have a break, you give gifts people crave even more than money: your presence and your friendship. Spending time is a wonderful way of sharing with others.

Providing Expertise

Some of the time you spend with others will be spent simply being available or doing tasks that anyone could accomplish. But you probably have another resource to provide in the form of skill or expertise in a particular subject area. When you provide that as a service to others, you help them in at least two ways: First, you almost certainly save them money because they would likely have to pay someone else for that capability. Second, you offer freedom and peace of mind because they are likely seeking help in a time of crisis.

An elderly person whose furnace breaks down faces a big problem. On a fixed income, they may be panicked about how to survive the winter. Your donation of expertise as an HVAC technician both saves money and provides tremendous peace of mind.

True, it can be annoying to be constantly solicited for free professional advice or services. School teachers are usually the first ones asked to lead a small group at church. Accountants are always nominated for treasurer of their club or committee. Auto mechanics, doctors, and lawyers get called frequently by friends and acquaintances who want to "pick their brain" for a minute. You'll likely need to set some commonsense limits on the amount of time you spend giving free services. Yet be generous in sharing your expertise. You almost certainly have knowledge, skill, experience, or talents that could benefit someone else. When you freely share with others, you open your hand to the world. The world will open its hand to you in return.

Offering Ideas and Information

Sometimes scarcity thinking reveals itself in our attitude toward the intangible resources we hold, including ideas. We may hoard ideas and information, especially at work, because doing so brings us a greater sense of security. For example, if you're the only one who knows where all the fire extinguishers are located, or how to balance the books at month's end, or how to prepare the order for an important client, then your place in the company seems more secure.

We may hoard ideas too, fearing that if we give away our best concepts, others will succeed ahead of us. That's classic scarcity thinking applied to knowledge rather than tangible resources.

Your willingness to share ideas and information is a clear signal that you've adopted an abundance mind-set, and it's a key way of being generous with others. Contrary to your intuition, giving these things away actually multiplies both the ideas and your value to others. When you are the only one who understands a process, people feel forced to deal with you. But when you teach them how a complicated system works, they will see you as an expert and begin to seek your counsel. When you hold on to a concept until you have a chance to develop it, you slow the momentum in your department. But when you hand out good ideas like jelly beans, you become the go-to person for creative solutions.

Be generous with your ideas. Share information as widely as you can. Your generosity will be rewarded with influence.

Sharing Relationships

Relationships are another intangible resource that can be generously shared. As with ideas and information, we may be tempted to hoard our most valuable relationships precisely because they mean so much to us. After all, you don't want to lose a valuable client, and adding another person to your mentoring group would seem to diminish your role in it. But relationships, like ideas, multiply when they are shared. Love, friendship, and camaraderie are infinite resources. There is always room for one more person in your heart, and likely at the dinner table or in your circle of friends.

Never be afraid to make a referral, provide an introduction, or offer an invitation. Connectors—people who have a reputation for bringing others together—are always valued acquaintances. When you are generous in including new people into your circle or introducing acquaintances to one another, both sides will value your friendship all the more. It is true that not every personality fits into every social structure, such as a team or work group or support group. But don't allow fear of a misfit or fear of loss to prevent you from trying. You don't lose a friend when you share that friend with others. You gain more. Connectors are influencers.

Giving Credit

Credit, meaning affirmation or praise for the things you have done, is yet another intangible you may be tempted to hoard. But it is better when shared.

Everyone likes to be praised, and we all enjoy being noticed or rewarded for our achievements. That can lead us to gather as much acclaim as we can for ourselves and avoid doling out any credit to others. But when you are generous in affirming others, you'll find that the principle of abundance operates in this area as well. The more you praise others, the more likely you are to be affirmed for the things you do. It's not that you should praise others with a mercenary motive. You simply understand that the world rewards generosity.

When you receive recognition or an award for any achievement, share the credit with those who helped you succeed. Be like an Academy Award winner on Oscar night: thank everyone you can think of. They'll be grateful for the notice, and it will build trust and influence.

Be generous in praising others who succeed ahead of you, including other teammates, coworkers, family members, and fellow students—even competitors. They will be grateful for your recognition and will respect your humility. Be willing to forego the credit when your good ideas are attributed to someone else. It'll be an exercise in modesty. And besides, piping in with "But that was my idea!" appears cheap and ungracious. Generous people praise liberally. Be known as a generous person.

Lending Resources

Lending, donating, or sharing resources is another way to practice generosity. Many of us have more resources than we need at any given moment. For example, there is likely a set of tools in your garage you aren't using just now, and perhaps won't for several weeks or months. You could easily loan them to a friend, saving him or her the expense of a purchase.

Take a mental inventory of your attic, basement, closets, and spare room. What unused items do you see there? A typical home is likely to contain at least a few things that are seldom or never touched, such as a musical instrument, second television set, spare computer, toys, clothing, tools, bicycles, spare dishes, or perhaps even a car. When you share, lend, or donate such items, you meet another person's need out of your excess, the very definition of generosity. Unlike a donation of money, a loaned item will likely be returned, allowing you to be generous over and over with the same resource.

Think for a moment about the needs that may exist within your social network. Some of those needs are likely temporary. Do you have an item that might meet a need for someone else? And what items do you have that you will likely never use again? Could you donate them to an individual or worthy organization?

Make generosity a part of your lifestyle. Don't fear that others will think of your garage contents as their personal inventory. You can easily deal with abusive practices if others take advantage of your kindness. Remember: "Give, and it will be given to you."[6]

Offering Hospitality

Hospitality is an all-but-forgotten form of generosity in American culture. Though a prized virtue in some other lands, many of us in the

United States have relegated hospitality almost entirely to the industry of hotels, restaurants, and catering. Yet hospitality is so much more than offering someone a place to stay or a meal. It is welcoming strangers into your presence, wherever that may be. It is seeing to the needs of others—including their needs for refreshment and lodging—ahead of your own.

One way of providing hospitality is to host someone for a meal or to provide them a place to stay. Another is to welcome a newcomer into your workplace, school, or other social setting. Remember that any first-timer will have certain needs or questions and may feel out of place. You can be hospitable by offering a new student a tour of the school, by orienting a new employee to office procedures, or by showing a new neighbor the best places to shop. You can also practice hospitality by making sure each person in the breakroom is included in the conversation, or ensuring that nobody gets left behind when a group goes out for lunch.

Offering hospitality is not only a kind thing to do but also a powerful influencer, as my friend Heather discovered. When the administrators of her graduate studies program asked if anyone would temporarily host a newly arriving international student, Heather quickly volunteered—the only one in her program to do so. She and her husband provided accommodations, meals, and transportation to the student while he became oriented to a new country. They also arranged housing for the student and his wife, who would arrive later.

Though this student was from a culture that highly valued hospitality, he was surprised to encounter such generosity—including the use of a car—among Americans. "Heather," he asked in a slightly puzzled tone, "why are you doing this?" That question opened the door to a wonderful conversation about culture, worldview, and faith, and it was the beginning of an ongoing friendship between the two families.

When you share your welcome with others, you gain respect, trust, and influence in their lives.

SLEEPING WELL

Juan Antonio "Chi Chi" Rodriguez was one of the most colorful characters in the sport of golf during the more than two decades he was a fixture on the PGA circuit. He won eight major tournament titles and went on to play in the Senior PGA Tour. Besides winning, the diminutive Puerto Rican was known for two things: his quick wit and his generous spirit.

As a young boy, Rodriguez worked in the sugar cane fields—his help was needed because there were six children in the family to feed. When the boy realized he could make more money as a caddie at a local golf club, he took a job there and became hooked on the game. As a grown man, after achieving success on the PGA tour, Rodriguez never forgot the struggles of his early life, and he never lost his heart for those in need. Though he had experienced scarcity, he lived by an abundance mind-set. He recalled, "My father would give his dinner to any hungry kids who walked by and then go in the backyard and pick weeds from the yard to eat. Everything I ever had I have shared. If you worry about giving, you will never have enough, of anything."[7]

Years later Rodriguez ran into financial problems. He joked, "I was making $37,000 and spending $100,000 on the poor. But so what? God forget [*sic*] to tell me how to say no." Thankfully, today, he and the Chi Chi Rodriguez Youth Foundation, which he founded in 1979, are doing well.[8] The voluble golfer summed up his approach to life this way: "Takers eat well, but givers sleep well."[9]

Generosity is a lifestyle. When you are generous with others, that liberality is rewarded in trust, respect, and influence. The world repays in kind. Givers receive more. Hoarders receive less. Be a giver, and opportunity will follow you.

Generosity is not a leadership tactic. It is a lifestyle of openness toward others and a freedom in spending your time, talent, and treasure for those in need. When you are generous with others, you'll find meaning in life and a sense of peace that may have eluded you before. As Rodriguez noted, "Givers sleep well."[10]

THE KEY THREE

1. Survey your attitudes and habits regarding generosity. Do you tend to have a scarcity mind-set or an attitude of abundance?

2. Name your chief obstacle to practicing generosity, then state what you will do to confront that objection or fear.

3. List three people in your social network who might benefit from your generosity. Choose at least one person to share with today.

THE POWER OF
YOUR COMMITMENT

Difficulties are just things to overcome, after all.

ERNEST SHACKLETON[1]

The 1968 Olympic Games in Mexico City were memorable for a number of reasons, one being the extreme altitude of the venue. At 7,350 feet above sea level, the altitude had a noticeable effect on the athletes. In sprints and short-distance races, the thinner air allowed for record-shattering performances. However, that same atmosphere caused a hardship for distance runners, who labored to draw every breath. Competitors in the men's marathon, the ultimate test of endurance, suffered the most. When the race began at 3:00 p.m. on October 20, the last day of the track and field competition, 75 athletes representing 41 countries set out from the Plaza de la Constitución on the 26.2-mile course. Only 57 runners would finish the race.

Defending champion Abebe Bikila would have been the favorite, having grown up in Addis Ababa, Ethiopia, which sits at an even higher altitude than Mexico City. But Bikila was handicapped by a stress fracture and was recovering from a recent appendectomy. Attention turned to Mamo Wolde, another Ethiopian who had trained at these same altitudes and competed in both the 1956 and 1964 Olympics. But Belgium's Gaston Roelants held the lead at the 12-mile mark, and Kenya's Naftali Temu edged ahead near mile 16. Meanwhile, 3 runners, including Wolde, were poised for a challenge.

Yet the real drama in the race was unfolding miles behind the lead group. John Stephen Akhwari was one of many competitors who struggled to compete in the thin air of Mexico City. Halfway through the race, Akhwari was among a group of runners vying for position when he was knocked to the pavement. Akhwari suffered a wound to his shoulder, plus the dislocation of his right knee. Incredibly, after receiving medical treatment, the intrepid Tanzanian elected to continue running. Far ahead on the course, Mamo Wolde had indeed taken the lead and gone on to win, a full three minutes ahead of the second-place runner. Meanwhile, John Stephen Akhwari limped on.

More than an hour later, 56 runners had finished the course and 18 more had dropped from the field. The sun had set on Mexico City, and most of the vast crowd had filed out of the stadium. Then word came in that a final runner was about to enter. Television cameras recorded the scene as Akhwari, limping along on his bandaged knee, finally crossed the finish line. He had been running for three hours and twenty-five minutes under grueling conditions and with no prospect of earning a medal. Later, a reporter asked Akhwari why he had continued to run. He replied, "My country didn't send me to Mexico to start the race. They sent me here to finish."[2]

John Stephen Akhwari's story has inspired countless athletes and many others who have faced near-impossible odds. He embodies the concept of commitment. Commitment is a willingness to continue pursuing a goal even when it becomes difficult or costly to achieve.

Those who display a high degree of commitment are highly influential because people respect the willingness to remain steadfast over the long term. In a world where it is easier than ever to quit one endeavor and begin another, those who remain committed to their vision, especially through times of adversity, become strong influencers. In this chapter, you will gain a firm motivation to remain engaged in the process of change despite the obstacles that may come your way. You will learn to harness the power of commitment.

WHY WE WALK AWAY

Quitting is easy, which is why so many people do it every day. That is not to say that those who abandon a goal—whether it is finishing school, remaining married, or starting a new business—are somehow soft or inferior. On the contrary, most of the people I've known who walked away from some pursuit were wonderful people who tried very hard to succeed. When I say that quitting is easy, I simply mean it's easier to quit than to remain committed to a goal in the face of adversity. Perhaps it would be more accurate to say that commitment is difficult.

And that is why commitment is such a powerful influence on others. We have all faced situations in which we gave our best, so far as we understood it at the time, but came up short. Rather than regroup and try again, we decided the goal was not worth the getting and let it slip away. So when we see a person who has been married for 50 years, or has maintained a successful business, or has finished a college degree, we admire their ability to persevere. We respect their commitment.

Sadly, most people quit just a bit too soon. None of us knows the future, so we cannot see how close we are to success. Those who have remained committed to their goals and achieved them almost always make some version of this statement: "I was on the verge of quitting when I had my big breakthrough," or, "I was ready to throw in the towel but decided to give it one more try; that's when success came." Like marathon runners who typically hit "the wall" around mile twenty, just six miles from the finish, visionaries in pursuit of any goal are likely to face their most discouraging moments when they are on the verge of success.

The reasons people back off on their dreams are complex, and it isn't simply because they lack character. Here are some reasons you may be tempted to abandon your dream too early. To understand them, we'll trace the stages every goal or project must go through to reach success: the launch, the climb, the dip, and the next phase.

Fear of Failure

Any project or goal typically involves four distinct phases. First is the launch, which includes planning, gathering resources, and making a start. This is the ribbon-cutting for a new business, the wedding ceremony, or the first day of classes in a new degree program. Everyone is excited on these occasions because the venture is fresh and filled with possibility. Whether it's a long van ride to Disney World or the first day of a new job, we all begin a new venture with eagerness. A few people, however, give up on the project right at the start. They abandon the project just at or before the launch. Why? Because they fear failure.

Sensing that it would be better to walk away now than to slog through weeks or years of frustration only to wind up with nothing, they back off at the very beginning. This is the groom who gets "cold feet" before the wedding. Is that caused by a genuine belief the marriage should not take place? Or is it simple fear that causes him to walk away? This is also the investor who pulls out at contract stage, or the homebuyer who walks away at the closing. In such cases, it is likely fear that caused them to abandon the goal: the fear of failure.

Eagerness Without Commitment

The second phase of any endeavor is the climb. That's when the hard work comes in. When the honeymoon is over—in a marriage or any other venture—discipline is needed in order to make this climb toward the goal. This is when you must stay up late and study for exams, get up early and go to work, or endure the daily grind of dealing with customers, changing diapers, or doing chores. The climb is hard work, and this is where those who were merely eager for the start of a project begin to fall away. Yes, they were eager for the goal. But they were not fully invested in achieving it. Eagerness will only carry you so far.

Loss of Hope

Many people are able to remain committed through the climb. The climb is hard work, but at least they are making slow and steady progress toward their goal. They can put up with the fatigue and frustrations because it seems that they're getting closer. They have the end in sight. Though it may take years of more work, they can remain committed because they know they're making progress.

Then comes the third stage in the life of any pursuit, which Seth Godin calls "the dip."[3] This stage comes after you've been climbing for a while. As the name implies, the dip is a downturn. Suddenly, everything changes. You start arguing more. You run short of money. You're more tired than you've ever been in your life. Customers complain. Coworkers walk out. Rather than slogging uphill, you find yourself cast down into a deep, dark valley. The goal now seems impossible. You question whether you have the ability to continue.

This moment is when most people abandon their dream. It's not hard work they're afraid of; it's failure. Calculating that the goal is now permanently beyond their resources and capacity to reach it, they choose to step back. Many people quit during this stage because they simply lose faith in the goal.

Inability to Pivot

Those who do remain committed through the dip generally find that something amazing happens. The hardship they face—the dip—becomes a critical element in their success. During this time of loss and confusion, they realize they must make adjustments in order to keep going.

In business, this may be called a *pivot*. This is when you decide that your snow removal company must become a landscape company if it is to survive. It's when you determine you'll need additional training, or more staff, or a fresh approach to fundraising in order to get your non-profit off the ground. It's when some couples realize they must accept one another's imperfections and forgive old hurts if they are to enter a new phase in their marriage.

Remarkably, the dip can be a necessary element for success because it forces the hard analysis and creative thinking that are necessary to solve problems. Those who can pivot—meaning they can make changes in themselves, their thinking, and their approach to the goal—can usually remain committed. Those who cannot pivot often fall away during the dip.

Lack of Personal Reserves

The fourth phase of the venture is, hopefully, the finish. This is the achievement of the goal: success in business, unity in marriage, completion of the degree, change in legislation, the publication of the book, or whatever the goal may be. The term *finish* may be misleading, however, because one goal often leads to another, and the cycle begins again. Successfully raising children leads to an empty nest, which is a new life stage with its own challenges. Success in business leads to the creation of wealth, which must then be properly managed.

Many people achieve their dream only to see it slip away later because they cannot remain committed through the finish of one project and the start of another. Often, the reason is that they lack the personal reserves to keep going. Though they may be creative thinkers, they need the personal discipline to manage their dream through its eventual success. They may become distracted, or lack self-confidence, or grow bored or tired. To remain committed to a goal beyond its completion and into the next phase of development requires a new level of commitment, one that many people are missing.

HOW TO DEVELOP COMMITMENT

If you have backed off on a goal before, you're not alone. The important thing is to learn from your experience. You really can remain committed far beyond the eagerness that causes you to launch your aspiration: through the difficulties of the long climb, past the inevitable dip, and even beyond the realization of your dream. It helps to understand the four phases of any project or venture. Besides that, here are five simple things you can do to develop your influence and stay committed to your dreams.

1. State Your Motivation

One of the most powerful ways to build your staying power on a vision, goal, or project is to clarify from the outset why this matters to you. When you understand your true purpose, you'll be better equipped to move from the initial flush of eagerness to the kind of true commitment that can weather the disappointments that are sure to come. Renowned Danish philosopher Søren Kierkegaard put it this way: "What matters is to find a purpose, to see what it really is that God wills that I shall do; the crucial thing is to find a truth which is truth for me, to find the idea for which I am willing to live and die."[4]

While your current vision for change may be less central to your true life's purpose, the more strongly you feel about your vision—the closer it is to your core values and beliefs—the more fully you'll be able to commit to it. Look for the link between the ways you are trying to influence others and your life's purpose. Write down a statement of your vision *and* why it matters so much to you. This statement is for your eyes only, so it need not be pretty or polished; only clear, concise, and meaningful to you. Establish in your own mind the importance and urgency of your vision, and your commitment will remain strong throughout the life cycle of your dream.

2. Recall Your Goal Weekly

Once you have taken the time to write down your vision, stating your motivation for achieving your goal, place that statement where you'll be sure to see it regularly. Don't tuck it in a notebook, slide it into a desk drawer, or allow it to get buried in a file on your computer. Make it your screen saver, tape it to the bathroom mirror, or place it wherever you keep your daily to-do list. It's crucial you see the statement often and review it purposefully at least once a week.

Muhammad Ali was known for his flamboyant style, including the pronouncement of himself as "The Greatest." No one can claim, however, that he was not an outstanding boxer and a great champion. Ali was blessed with amazing natural talents, but that was not the only ingredient in his success. According to a Twitter post, he later recalled, "I hated every minute of training, but I said, 'Don't quit. Suffer now and live the rest of your life as a champion.'"[5] Keeping his purpose squarely before him enabled the "Champ" to endure the long climb of physical training and, I'm sure, the dip of his first-ever career loss to Joe Frazier, a loss he made good in a rematch.

Remind yourself of your purpose frequently. It will solidify your commitment.

3. Seek a Support Community

Our culture tends to idolize the lone-wolf character: that strong, independent person who can persevere alone through all odds. That makes for a nice movie hero, but in real life everyone needs a support network in order to face adversity. You'll be far more likely to maintain your commitment if you surround yourself with a community of supporters. These are encouragers, coworkers, and friends who share your commitment to your vision for change.

Don't have a support community? No problem. You can create one simply by asking people to join you. An old proverb holds that "a cord of three strands is not quickly broken."[6] That's another way of saying there is strength in numbers. If you go it alone, your own resolve will carry you only so far. But when you are allied with others who share your vision, it will strengthen your commitment, enabling you to remain steadfast in your aims to the very end.

4. Recognize Impossibilities

It's important to say a word here about the difference between obstacles and impossibilities. An obstacle is a hurdle to overcome, a difficulty to work through, a challenge to your commitment that you must face and resolve. Lack of funding is an obstacle. Opposition from key stakeholders is an obstacle. Your own need for rest, learning, or growth are obstacles. With some creative thinking, perseverance, and teamwork, most obstacles can be overcome. Obstacles do not prevent you from reaching your goal; they merely make it more difficult. Obstacles become a test of your commitment, but they should not break your resolve.

Some things, however, are not mere obstacles, but true impossibilities. You may have a dream of becoming president of the United States, and you may influence a number of people to join you in that pursuit. However, if you are not a "natural born citizen," are less than 35 years old, or have not lived in the country for at least 14 years, you can't serve as president. You are constitutionally ineligible. True, you could attempt to amend Article II, Section I, Clause 5 of the US Constitution, but for all intents and purposes, your election is an impossibility.

Some impossibilities arise after you undertake to achieve your vision. You may face some obstacles—such as a lack of funding, physical limitations, or opposition from others—that are so monumental they render your dream an impossibility. Think of John Stephen Akhwari limping toward the finish line of the Olympic marathon. As the very last competitor on the course, still running even after the medals had been awarded, his original goal of winning the race had become an impossibility. What do you do when you face not obstacles, but impossibilities?

In such cases you have two choices. One is to discontinue the pursuit of your goal. In many instances, that is the wisest thing to do. Commitment is not the same as insanity, after all. There is no shame in abandoning a goal that is no longer possible to achieve, or for which the costs have simply become too great.

Sometimes, however, there is merit in remaining committed even in the face of impossible odds. Akhwari's dedication in finishing a race he could not possibly win has been an inspiration to many. Often, political candidates or other advocates for change will continue their campaign even when winning has become an impossibility. Their continued efforts draw attention to the worthiness of their cause.

Whatever your choice, make it with eyes wide open. Understand when your obstacles have become impossibilities. Be realistic about your circumstances. Whether you choose to abandon your vision or to carry on for the sake of principle, do so fully aware of the outcome you face.

5. Don't Quit

Notice that even in the face of an impossibility, we do not quit, but rather make the choice to abandon the pursuit of a goal. Is that mere semantics? Not really. Quitting always carries with it the idea of being beaten. It is giving up on something you really want to achieve but simply cannot pay the price to attain. Quitting is always a defeat, which is why those who do so seldom command respect, while valiant "losers" like Akhwari are esteemed for their sacrifice. Soldiers who surrender rather than cause further bloodshed when faced with inevitable defeat are not deserters. We make a distinction between those who quit based on fear and those who make a deliberate choice to discontinue. Don't quit.

KEEP GOING

Few athletes in recent memory have been both as inspiring and as controversial as Lance Armstrong, the cyclist who was stripped of his seven Tour de France championships for admitting to using performance-enhancing drugs. Regardless of those failings, Armstrong has been a hero to many because of his courageous fight against cancer. He is not only a cancer survivor, but has become a tireless advocate for cancer research. In a book about his comeback to the sport of cycling after treatment for testicular cancer, Armstrong wrote,

> Pain is temporary. It may last a minute, or an hour, or a day, or a year, but eventually it will subside and something else will take its place. If I quit, however, it lasts forever. That surrender, even the smallest act of giving up, stays with me. So when I feel like quitting, I ask myself, which would I rather live with? Facing up to that question, and finding a way to go on, is the real reward.[7]

You face the same question and the same potential for reward. The obstacles you meet in the pursuit of your dream are almost certainly temporary. Will you allow those short-term setbacks or hardships to take your eyes away from your goal, the positive change you hope to make in the world? Or will you face up to that question, finding a way to keep your commitment strong, and going on to see the realization of your dream?

Everyone has backed off on a goal at some time or other, so if you quit when things are difficult few will blame you. You might, however, bring regrets upon yourself that will be difficult to live with later on. If you are able to remain committed to your dream through thick and thin, you will find that something amazing happens. Like Akhwari, limping toward the finish line, you will begin to hear the cheers of those who applaud your commitment. They will respect you more highly and follow you more willingly because they see the strength of your resolve.

Whatever good goal you are pursuing, don't quit. Think of the finish line and remember all the reasons you chose to pursue this change in the world. Become inspired again by your dream for the future, and keep going.

THE KEY THREE

1. Recall the four stages of an endeavor and determine which stage you are in now.

2. What obstacles might you face in achieving your goals? What resources do you have—or can obtain—for overcoming them?

3. Write out your motivation for the change you hope to see in the world. If you have already written this statement, review it now.

THE POWER OF YOUR SACRIFICE

*Each time a man stands up for an ideal, or acts
to improve the lot of others, or strikes out against
injustice, he sends forth a tiny ripple of hope.*

ROBERT F. KENNEDY[1]

My father, William Aaron Toler, was one of the greatest men I've ever known. Though he died when I was just 11 years old, his life was dedicated to serving his family. He began his working life as a coal miner in McDowell County, West Virginia, the most productive coal region in the state but one of the poorest counties in the nation. Dad worked every day in the mines, returning home tired, his face blackened with coal soot. Our tiny home in Baileysville provided just enough shelter for our family of five. Because Dad worked underground all day, he seldom saw daylight, especially during the winter months. Mining is a perilous occupation, and Dad broke his back three times in the mines while laboring to feed our family. More than once I saw him cough up black coal dust into a snow-white handkerchief, a common occurrence among miners of that day.

Realizing that his family's welfare depended on his own health, Dad chose to move our family to Columbus, Ohio, in search of a better life. Things didn't improve immediately though, and he went several months without finding work. Even so, Dad's attitude was always bright. We ate a lot of pinto beans and fried bologna, but we were happy.

Eventually Dad did find a job with a construction company, and we were all elated. I know it felt good to my father to be employed again, and the whole family was excited to have a bit more money for food and occasional treats. Dad was working, Mom was content, and my brothers and I were doing well in our new school. Everything seemed to be back to normal—actually, better than the "normal" we had known up to that point.

Then one Monday morning Dad went to work and never came home. Having escaped the harrowing dangers of the coal mine, he was electrocuted in a tragic on-the-job accident.

I recall many lessons my father taught me during our few years together: the value of hard work, how to save money, the blessings of faith and family, the power of a positive attitude. Yet the most important lesson I learned from Dad was the power of sacrifice.

Dad worked hard at the risk of his own health and life, but he did not do it for himself. His goal was never to enjoy luxuries or to advance his own name. Dad toiled day in and day out to provide for his family and to support our local church. He did it for us. He did it for God. And he never complained. He was cheerful even in the direst circumstances. Why? Dad was hopeful by nature, but it was more than that. He realized that he was the leader in our home and was responsible for our well-being. He would not allow himself to be dispirited because he knew how it would affect the rest of us.

I have been privileged to know many great people during my lifetime. I've had the opportunity to learn from pastors and statesmen, great athletes and powerful business executives—the kind of people who create tremendous impact on the lives of others. Yet I can honestly say that no human being has been a greater influence in my life than my father. That was not because he was wealthy or powerful, highly educated or extremely successful. It was because of the power of his sacrifice on behalf of his family and his faith.

Generosity is sharing from abundance. Sacrifice is giving at a level that risks loss. Generosity results in gratitude, but sacrifice produces devotion. Sacrifice leads to the most powerful influence because it is a demonstration of love. The influence of Mahatma Gandhi, Dr. Martin

Luther King Jr., Bill Bright, and other great leaders endures precisely because they were willing to put the needs of others ahead of their own.

In this chapter, you will learn the power of sacrifice. You will be inspired to give the greatest possible gift to others: yourself.

SACRIFICES THAT IMPACT OTHERS

Human beings are naturally inclined to put themselves first. Though we all have nobler moments, our first instinct is to place our own wants and needs ahead of others' wants and needs. This is the urge you have to take the largest piece of pie for yourself, to step on the gas when you see another driver approaching the same intersection, or to think, "I wish that was me," when someone else receives an award or recognition. This impulse for self-promotion is one of the most basic aspects of human nature. Though we recognize that it must be held in check, and we may be largely successful at doing so, the impulse never really goes away.

That's why acts of personal sacrifice are so compelling. When we see another person set aside their desire for self-protection, self-promotion, or self-preservation in order to benefit others, we are truly impressed. For example, when we see a video of a man wading into rushing flood-waters to save a child, or when we hear of a person who donates a kidney to a friend or shares their last bit of food, something inside us says, "Wow." We find ourselves hoping that we would do the same in similar circumstances, but we're not sure. Selfless sacrifice is one of the few things that garners universal respect. And that's exactly why it is such a powerful influencer. When others see that you are genuinely more concerned for their well-being than for your own, they will esteem you highly and listen to you closely.

As with the other influence builders mentioned in this book, self-sacrifice is not a mere tool for gaining attention. Faux altruism is usually easy to spot and winds up having the opposite effect. People disrespect those who use the appearance of concern to manipulate their emotions. We should sacrifice for the needs of others because it's the right thing to do, not because we hope to gain from it. At the same time, it's helpful to recognize the ways in which our sacrifice enables us to influence others for the common good. When you place others ahead of yourself in these key areas, you gain a greater ability to influence them for good.

Surrendering Your Power

The first way we can sacrifice for others is in the area of power, which can be defined in terms of rights, privileges, and control of circumstances. Though you may not feel like a powerful person, each of us has a certain amount of power in all our social contexts. We have rights as citizens. We enjoy privileges based on our family relationships or social status. And we hold some power in our social relationships and employment. Our instinct is to cling to our privileges and power, and to enhance them whenever possible. We are competitive by nature, we vie for promotions, and we are eager to gain special privileges that set us apart from others. So when we go against that urge and voluntarily surrender power on behalf of others, it establishes our leadership and influence.

Nelson Mandela was president of South Africa from 1994 to 1999, but he is perhaps better known as a crusader against apartheid who spent 27 years in prison. At his sentencing in 1964, he faced possible execution for his conviction on charges of treason. Prior to the pronouncement of his sentence, Mandela made this statement:

> During my lifetime I have dedicated myself to this struggle of the African people. I have fought against white domination, and I have fought against black domination. I have cherished the ideal of a democratic and free society in which all persons live together in harmony and with equal opportunities. It is an ideal which I hope to live for and to achieve. But if needs be, it is an ideal for which I am prepared to die.[2]

Mandela proved the power of his conviction through the sacrifice of his freedom. Decades later, he was released from prison and apartheid came to an end. In 1994, he was elected the first black head of state in South Africa.

However, Mandela served only a single term in that office. Having launched an effort at national reconciliation, he believed that a good foundation had been set for the future. Although he was eligible for another five-year term, Mandela chose to walk away from the power he had worked so long to achieve because he believed it to be in the best interest of the country.[3] That act cemented his legacy as a leader who was willing to put the needs of others ahead of his own privilege and power. That kind of sacrifice is rare and always revered. We find it astounding when someone voluntarily surrenders their rights, privileges, or power on behalf of others.

You may never have the occasion to sacrifice power in such a grand way, but you will certainly face occasions when you have the choice to hold on to your rights or to surrender them to meet the needs of others. When you choose to forgive another person, you sacrifice your right for personal justice or compensation—and when you do that as an act of mercy or compassion, you gain rather than lose respect. When you strike a compromise with an employee or coworker that allows their agenda to advance, you may surrender a bit of the control that was due to you. Yet when others see you have put the needs of the group ahead of your own career or reputation, your influence will grow. Even simple acts such as allowing a person to enter ahead of you or to take a parking spot that could have been yours enhance your leadership.

Notice two aspects of this surrender of privilege or power: it is done voluntarily and for the sake of others. This is not submitting to the victimization perpetrated by others in order to advance themselves. That kind of injustice is not to be tolerated. We are speaking here of the willing surrender of your rights in order to meet the genuine needs of another. When you put others first, they will notice. And when they have a genuine need, your gift will not be seen as a sign of weakness, but of strength. Your influence will grow as a result.

Transferring Your Wealth

A second area in which we may sacrifice ourselves for the benefit of others is in the use of our wealth. Few of us feel as if we are wealthy, but we are. If you are reading this book, chances are good that you have enough disposable income to buy the book and enough spare time to read it. In a world in which an estimated three billion people live in poverty,[4] requiring all their time and energy be devoted to gaining enough food to survive, those two facts indicate you have wealth. And it's possible you have even more resources than that. One definition of wealth is excess, so if you have more food, money, clothing, and resources than you need to survive, by that definition you are wealthy. Since we all value wealth—which is usually reckoned in terms of money—very highly, those who are willing to give money away, especially when it changes their own financial status, are rare indeed.

Warren Buffett, one of the wealthiest people on earth, made headlines when he announced that he would give away nearly all his fortune. The highly successful investor has a vision for giving back to society, and he elected to do so by granting the bulk of his money to philanthropic causes—notably the Bill & Melinda Gates Foundation, which is active in improving health care and reducing poverty worldwide. The total value of Buffett's planned gifts, to be given over a period of years, was calculated at some $37 billion, an astoundingly generous amount by any standard, and possibly the largest sum ever given away. The gift—if given all at once—would have reduced the value of Buffett's fortune (in Berkshire Hathaway stock) to *only* $6.8 billion.[5]

Buffett's gift sets a marvelous example for others to follow, and we must note that he also pledged to donate the remainder of his wealth by the time of his death.[6] We should all use our resources to impact the world in such positive ways.

While Buffett's example powerfully illustrates generosity, he is giving out of his abundance. As someone has aptly put it, the true measure of your sacrifice is not how much you give, but how much you have left after you give. Generosity is impressive; sacrifice is extraordinary.

Jesus, the greatest teacher of all time, illustrated this point while watching people make donations to a religious institution. Observing many wealthy people giving large gifts, he also noticed a poor woman who put in two copper coins—essentially two cents. And he said, "This poor widow has put in more than all the others. All these people gave their gifts out of their wealth; but she out of her poverty put in all she had to live on."[7]

As a boy, I saw countless examples of this very same sacrificial giving. Poor as our family was, my father always insisted we boys take a few cents with us to church to put in the offering plate. Dad knew that some of the money went to help families who were even harder hit than we were. And when things were at their worst for the Toler household, we received a gift of groceries from folks at the church. Some of them had barely enough to eat themselves, yet they were willing to share with others.

When you give sacrificially to benefit others, whether it is to a food program, an educational initiative, or a fight for justice, you demonstrate that your own status means less to you than the welfare of others. When you donate to a scholarship fund while still paying off your own student loans, you demonstrate your commitment to doing good in the world. When you place a few food items in the collection box outside the supermarket despite the fact you're living paycheck to paycheck, you make a tangible sacrifice to benefit others. When you give to support a missionary, you forego buying certain things for yourself. When others see your dedication to helping others by sharing what you have, you gain respect in their eyes and the influence that goes along with it.

Risking Your Safety

A third area in which we may sacrifice for others is in risking our safety for their care or survival. Though there have been many brave souls who have literally given up their lives to save another person—like Father Maximilian Kolbe, who volunteered to take the place of a condemned man at Auschwitz[8]—most of us will never be called upon to knowingly make such a sacrifice. However, there are many occasions on which we may place our wealth, reputation, or health at risk on behalf of others. Our willingness to disregard our own safety is a powerful statement of our concern for others, and that concern brings great respect.

On November 9, 2007, a group of soldiers was en route from the village of Aranas, Afghanistan, to their remote combat outpost. They had hoped to spend the day meeting with a group of village elders, but the soldiers suspected trouble when the elders delayed the meeting for several hours and an unusually large group of villagers turned out for the meeting. Some of the villagers trailed the soldiers toward their outpost, then launched an attack. Sgt. Kyle White began to engage the attackers but was rendered unconscious by a rocket-propelled grenade. As he awoke, an enemy round exploded near his head, sending shrapnel into his face.

Shaking off his wounds, Sgt. White noticed a fellow soldier who had been shot in the arm. Without hesitation, Sgt. White moved to help the soldier, exposing himself to enemy fire in the process. He then went to help an injured marine, offering aid until the man died from his wounds. After, Sgt. White returned to help the other soldier—again under heavy enemy fire—who had been shot a second time. Sgt. White applied a tourniquet that stopped the bleeding.

Realizing that both his radio and his comrade's radio were broken, Sgt. White braved enemy fire yet again to retrieve a radio from the deceased marine. With it, he provided information that allowed friendly forces to make air strikes that subdued the enemy attack and called for medical evacuation of his fellow soldiers, marines, and Afghan Army soldiers.

For displaying extraordinary heroism and selflessness by risking his own life for others, Sgt. Kyle J. White was awarded the Medal of Honor, his country's highest award for bravery. Sgt. White later recalled thinking, "It's just a matter of time before I'm dead. If that's going to happen, I might as well help someone while I can."[9, 10, 11] That attitude exemplifies not only the heroism of a Medal of Honor recipient but also the attitude of all who risk their comfort and security for the benefit of others.

Opportunities to display heroic, life-endangering selflessness are rare in wartime and rarer in civilian life. Yet we all have occasion to leave the safety and comfort of our own lives behind in order to benefit others. When you take up the call for justice on behalf of the oppressed, you risk your reputation and possibly sacrifice the comfortable life you've been used to. When you decide to promote change in your home or workplace, you leave the comfort zone of conformity. When you do that not merely for your own interests, but also to better the lives of others, you make a sacrifice that's worth noting. When you risk your health, wealth, comfort, or reputation in order to advance the well-being of those around you, you merit their respect.

As Sgt. White said, "When you're deployed, those people become your family. What you really care about is: I want to get this guy to the left and to the right home."[12] When the welfare of the people on your left and right becomes as important to you as your own well-being, you will have earned the right to be an influencer in their lives.

EVERYDAY HERO

Civil rights leaders, billionaires, Medal of Honor recipients. Having read this chapter, you might conclude that only extraordinary sacrifices of courage, generosity, or heroism are worthy of respect. Not so. Every day, ordinary folks like you and me make the unexceptional sacrifices that make a home, classroom, office, or neighborhood better than they were before.

When a dad like mine goes to work every day, risking his own health for the security of his children, he leaves a powerful legacy. When a student gives up his time to tutor another student, helping them succeed, she makes a sacrifice worth remembering. When a teacher or employer, mom or mentor, classmate or coworker sacrifices time, contributes money, risks their reputation, or moves out of their comfort zone not to make themselves a star, but to provide for the needs of others, we all are richer for it.

Every day, you have opportunities large and small to sacrifice yourself on behalf of others. There is no question about whether or not your sacrifice will be worthwhile, or whether or not it will be rewarded with increased esteem, respect, and attention. It certainly will be. The only question is this: Will you live your life for Christ and others, or only for yourself? Your answer to that question will, in large measure, determine the level of your influence.

· · · · · · · · · · · · · · · **THE KEY THREE** · · · · · · · · · · · · · ·

1. Name the person you most respect, then state what you
   have seen them sacrifice for others.

2. Review the three areas in which we often make sacrifices for others, and name the one that you find most challenging. Discuss this finding with a friend or mentor.

3. Name the most pressing need you see within your family, church, school, neighborhood, or workplace. Now ask God what you should sacrifice in order to meet that need.

Afterword:

YOU CAN!

Let's go back to the beginning. At the start of this book, I asked you to state your vision for the world, the positive change you hope to make in your home, community, workplace, or even your nation. This vision is the reason you want to be an influencer in the first place. Take a moment to review that positive change. Call it to mind. Literally envision it. What will the world look like when you succeed in influencing others to change? It's an inspiring picture, isn't it?

Yet it is not without challenges. By now you've realized that achieving this vision will not be easy. Perhaps it seems too big for you to tackle. You may be wondering, "What have I gotten myself into?" If so, you're not alone. Everyone who envisions a better world faces that moment of apprehension, and that's the way it should be. If your vision seems within easy reach, it's too small to be worthy of your commitment and sacrifice. Every worthwhile dream seems a bit terrifying at the start. But take courage. You *can* do this. You can influence the world. The leap from where you are now to your vision for the future may seem great, but you can bridge the gap.

Remember that influencing others is a long game. This is a marathon, not a sprint. It will take months or even years to draw others toward your positive vision. And remember that your influence begins within yourself. If you hope to influence others, you must first gain control of yourself—your thoughts, attitudes, and actions. If you don't know where to begin, start there. You must become the change you hope to see in the world.

Next you will influence others through your vision, thoughts, words, habits, presence, encouragement, and generosity—and through the compelling power of your commitment and sacrifice. If you are diligent, your influence will not stop there. Through those with whom you come into contact, your vision will ripple outward, affecting more and more people over time. Ultimately, you will change the world.

Impossible? No. This result is entirely possible if you are able to harness the incredible power of your personal impact. Remember, you are influencing others all the time, whether you are aware of it or not. And that influence is never neutral. You constantly affect others in either negative or positive ways. When you are able to seize that power and harness it to further your vision, nothing can stop you from achieving your goal.

I believe in you! I am convinced you have what it takes to gain mastery of yourself, influence others, and impact the world. Only one question remains for you to answer: When will you begin?

NOTES

INTRODUCTION: THE POWER TO CHANGE THE FUTURE

1. Ken Blanchard and Phil Hodges, *Servant Leader: Transforming your Heart, Head, Hands and Habits* (Nashville: Thomas Nelson, 2003), 10.

2. Loren Eiseley, "The Star Thrower" as found in *The Unexpected Universe* (New York: Harcourt, 1969).

3. Michael Karson, "Punishment Doesn't Work," *Psychology Today*, January 14, 2014, https://www.psychologytoday.com/blog/feeling-our-way/201401/punishment-doesnt-work.

4. Martin Luther King Jr., "I Have a Dream," *American Rhetoric: Top 100 Speeches*, accessed February 7, 2017, http://www.americanrhetoric.com/speeches/mlkihaveadream.htm.

CHAPTER 1: THE NATURE OF INFLUENCE

1. Ralph Waldo Emerson, *The Conduct of Life* (Boston: Houghton Mifflin, 1860), 258.

2. Zig Ziglar, "Little Things Make a Big Difference: The Choice Is Yours," *AdvantEdge Newsletter*, 2013, http://www.nightingale.com/newsletters/zig-ziglar-little-things-make-a-big-difference-the-choice-is-yours-577/.

3. Howard Zinn, *You Can't Be Neutral on a Moving Train*, a documentary released in 2004.

4. Ezekiel 22:29-30.

CHAPTER 2: THREE DIMENSIONS OF INFLUENCE

1. John C. Maxwell, *The 5 Levels of Leadership: Proven Steps to Maximize Your Potential* (New York: Center Street, 2011), 44.

2. The Associated Press, "The Latest: Melenchon Is in 7 Places at Once, With Hologram," *The New York Times*, April 18, 2017, https://www.nytimes.com/aponline/2017/04/18/world/europe/ap-eu-france-election-the-latest.html (article no longer available).

3. The Associated Press, "French Candidate Uses Hologram to Travel Campaign Trail," *U.S. News & World Report*, February 5, 2017, https://www.usnews.com/news/world/articles/2017-02-05/french-candidate-uses-hologram-to-travel-campaign-trail.

4. See Colossians 3:9-10.

5. 1 Timothy 3:5.

6. Eliott C. McLaughlin, "Man Dragged off United Flight Has Concussion, Will File Suit, Lawyer Says," *CNN*, April 14, 2017, http://www.cnn.com/2017/04/13/travel/united-passenger-pulled-off-flight-lawsuit-family-attorney-speak/.

7. Brad Tuttle, "Warren Buffett's Boring, Brilliant Wisdom," *Time*, March 1, 2010, http://business.time.com/2010/03/01/warren-buffetts-boring-brilliant-wisdom/.

8. Jon Ronson, "How One Stupid Tweet Blew Up Justine Sacco's Life," *The New York Times*, February 12, 2015, https://www.nytimes.com/2015/02/15/magazine/how-one-stupid-tweet-ruined-justine-saccos-life.html.

9. "About Anne Frank" at Anne Frank Center for Mutual Respect, http://annefrank.com/about-anne-frank/.

10. Anne Frank, *The Diary of a Young Girl*, trans. B. M. Mooyaart-Doubleday (New York: Bantam, 1993), 197.

11. Anne Frank, *Anne Frank's Tales from the Secret Annex*, trans. Ralph Manheim and Michel Mok (Garden City: Doubleday, 1984), 131.

12. Frank, *Anne Frank's Tales from the Secret Annex.*

CHAPTER 3: THE POWER OF YOUR VISION

1. Walt Disney, as quoted in Pat Williams with Jim Denney, *How to Be Like Walt: Capturing the Disney Magic Every Day of Your Life* (Deerfield Beach: Health Communications, 2004), 69.

2. Harry Readhead, "This Train Driver Got on the Wrong Service and Then Set Off in the Wrong Direction," *Metro*, April 9, 2015, http://metro.co.uk/2015/04/09/this-train-driver-got-on-the-wrong-service-and-then-set-off-in-the-wrong-direction-5141303/.

3. "How Does GPS Work?" *NASA Space Place*, May 6, 2015, https://spaceplace.nasa.gov/gps/en/.

4. Martin Luther King, Jr., "I Have a Dream…," *National Archives*, 1963, https://www.archives.gov/files/press/exhibits/dream-speech.pdf.

5. John F. Kennedy, "Excerpt from an Address Before a Joint Session of Congress, 25 May 1961," *John F. Kennedy Presidential Library and Museum*, May 25, 1961, https://www.jfklibrary.org/Asset-Viewer/xzwlgaeeTES6khED14P1Iw.aspx.

6. "Alzheimer's Association FY15–FY18 Strategic Plan," *Alzheimer's Association*, accessed May 23, 2017, http://www.alz.org/about_us_strategic_plan.asp.

7. "Our Purpose and Beliefs," *Oxfam International*, accessed May 23, 2017, https://www.oxfam.org/en/our-purpose-and-beliefs.

8. John C. Maxwell, "People Do What People See," *Bloomberg*, November 19, 2007, https://www.bloomberg.com/news/articles/2007-11-19/people-do-what-people-seebusinessweek-business-news-stock-market-and-financial-advice.

9. Andy Stanley, "Creating a Culture of Continual Improvement, Part 1," *The Andy Stanley Leadership Podcast*, podcast audio, March 3, 2017, https://itunes.apple.com/us/podcast/andy-stanley-leadership-podcast/id290055666?mt=2.

CHAPTER 4: THE POWER OF YOUR THOUGHTS

1. Bob Selden, "The Train Story—a Journey, an Experience, and a Feeling!" *A Gift of Inspiration*, accessed May 23, 2017, http://www.agiftofinspiration.com.au/stories/attitude/.

2. Barbara L. Fredrickson, "The Broaden-and-Build Theory of Positive Emotions," *The Royal Society*, August 17, 2004, 1367, https://www.ncbi.nlm.nih.gov/pmc/.

3. Fredrickson, 1367.

4. Fredrickson, 1375.

5. Luke 6:45.

6. Gottfried Wilhelm Leibniz, *Theodicy: Essays on the Goodness of God, the Freedom of Man and the Origin of Evil*, trans. E. M. Huggard (New York: Cosimo, 2009), 128.

7. Justin Kruger and David Dunning, "Unskilled and Unaware of It: How Difficulties in Recognizing One's Own Incompetence Lead to Inflated Self-Assessments," *Journal of Personality and Social Psychology* 77 (December 1999): 1121–1134.

8. Luke 6:38.

9. Robert H. Schuller, *Move Ahead with Possibility Thinking* (New York: Jove, 1978), 15.

10. George Bernard Shaw, as quoted in Robert F. Kennedy, "Remarks at the University of Kansas, March 18, 1968," *John F. Kennedy Presidential Library and Museum*, March 18, 1968, https://www .jfklibrary.org/Research/Research-Aids/Ready-Reference/RFK-Speeches/Remarks-of-Robert-F-Kennedy-at-the-University-of-Kansas-March-18-1968.aspx.

11. Kate Harkness, as cited in Robert Biswas-Diener and Todd B. Kashdan, "What Happy People Do Differently," *Psychology Today*, July 2, 2013, https://www.psychologytoday.com/articles/201307/ what-happy-people-do-differently.

CHAPTER 5: THE POWER OF YOUR WORDS

1. Ingrid Bengis, *Combat in the Erogenous Zone* (New York: Alfred A. Knopf, 1972), 46.

2. "The Power of Words," YouTube video, 1:47, *Purple Feather*, February 23, 2010, http://purple feather.co.uk/our-story.

3. See Matthew 7:3–5.

4. Proverbs 24:26.

5. Ann Landers, "Surrounded by Love, He Was Ready for a Miracle," *Chicago Tribune*, March 2, 1993, http://articles.chicagotribune.com/1993-03-02/features/9303186542_1_dear-ann-landers -diets-don-t-work-long-distance-truck-driver.

CHAPTER 6: THE POWER OF YOUR EXAMPLE

1. Henry David Thoreau, *Letters to a Spiritual Seeker*, ed. Bradley P. Dean (New York: W. W. Norton, 2004), 38.

2. As cited in Michelle Trudeau and Jane Greenhalgh, "Yawning May Promote Social Bonding Even Between between Dogs and Humans," Morning Edition, National Public Radio, May 15, 2017, http://www.npr.org/sections/health-shots/2017/05/15/527106576/yawning-may-pro mote-social-bonding-even-between-dogs-and-humans.

3. Brad Tuttle, "Warren Buffett's Boring, Brilliant Wisdom," *Time*, March 1, 2010, http://business. time.com/2010/03/01/warren-buffetts-boring-brilliant-wisdom/.

CHAPTER 7: THE POWER OF YOUR PRESENCE

1. Joe Gibbs, as quoted in "Joe Gibbs: Leaving a Legacy," *CBN*, http://www1.cbn.com/700club/joe-gibbs-leaving-legacy.http://www.npr.org/templates/story/story.php?storyId=5064534.

2. Debbie Hall, "The Power of Presence," NPR, December 26, 2005, https://www.npr.org/ templates/story/story.php?storyId=5064534.

3. Jo Anne Lyon, *The Ultimate Blessing: My Journey to Discover God's Presence* (Indianapolis: Wesleyan, 2009), 27.

4. Woody Allen, as quoted in Susan Braudy, "He's Woody Allen's Not-So-Silent Partner," *The New York Times Archives*, August 21, 1977, http://www.nytimes.com/1977/08/21/archives/hes-woody-allens-notsosilent-partner.html.

5. Matthew 7:12.

6. Barry Corey, "Loving Others through the Power of Presence," *Tyndale*, accessed June 8, 2017, https://www.tyndale.com/stories/the-power-of-presence.

CHAPTER 8: THE POWER OF YOUR ENCOURAGEMENT

1. Abigail Van Buren, "Exercise in Self-Esteem Is Lesson for a Lifetime," *Dear Abby*, *UExpress*, January 10, 1999, http://www.uexpress.com/dearabby/1999/1/10/exercise-in-self-esteem-is-lesson.

2. Garson O'Toole, "Be Kind; Everyone You Meet Is Fighting a Hard Battle," *Quote Investigator*, June 29, 2010, https://quoteinvestigator.com/2010/06/29/be-kind/.

3. Dale Carnegie, *How to Win Friends and Influence People*, rev. ed. (1936; repr., New York: Gallery, 1936), 227.

4. Ann Landers, "Simple Words Can Comfort," *Sun Sentinel*, December 30, 1993, http://articles.sun-sentinel.com/1993-12-30/lifestyle/9312290209_1_dear-ann-landers-new-jersey-woman-daughter.

CHAPTER 9: THE POWER OF YOUR GENEROSITY

1. These statements all appear in the same source, but not worded exactly this way as a single quotation. Nonetheless, they represent the essence of John Wesley's thinking on generosity. John Wesley, "The Use of Money," *The Works of John Wesley*, 3rd ed. (Kansas City: Beacon Hill, 1979), 126, 131, 133.

2. "Tom Bloch," *Big Think*, http://bigthink.com/experts/tombloch.

3. "A CEO Who Left His Family's Company to Follow His Heart," Donor Stories, *Greater Kansas City Community Foundation*, https://www.growyourgiving.org/donor-stories.

4. See at http://bigthink.com/experts/tombloch.

5. Luke 6:38.

6. See Luke 6:38.

7. "Quotes," Chi Chi Rodriguez, *Biography*, November 16, 2016, https://www.biography.com/people/chi-chi-rodriguez-189145.

8. See at https://www.biography.com/people/chi-chi-rodriguez-189145.

9. Chi Chi Rodriguez, as quoted in Bob Verdi, "Be Like Chi Chi: Be a Good Giver," *Chicago Tribune*, November 26, 1991, http://articles.chicagotribune.com/1991-11-26/sports/9104170126_1_chi-chi-rodriguez-new-york-yankees-front-agents.

10. See at http://articles.chicagotribune.com/1991-11-26/sports/9104170126_1_chi-chi-rodriguez-new-york-yankees-front-agents.

CHAPTER 10: THE POWER OF YOUR COMMITMENT

1. Ernest Shackleton, as quoted in Roland Huntford, *Shackleton* (New York: Carroll & Graf, 1985), 261.

2. "Athletics at the 1968 Ciudad de México Summer Games: Men's Marathon," *Sports Reference*, http://www.sports-reference.com/olympics/summer/1968/ATH/mens-marathon.html; "The Incredible Story of Tanzania's John-Stephen Akhwari - Mexico 1968 Olympics," YouTube video, :41, posted by "Olympic," May 1, 2013, https://www.youtube.com/watch?v=eNt_jynuAtI. See video description.

3. Seth Godin, *The Dip: A Little Book That Teaches You When to Quit (and When to Stick)* (New York: Portfolio, 2007), 4.

4. Søren Kierkegaard, "Gilleleie, August 1, 1835," *Søren Kierkegaard's Journals and Papers*, trans. and ed. Howard V. Hong and Edna H. Hong, vol. 5 (Bloomington: Indiana University, 1978), 34.

5. Muhammad Ali, Twitter post, April 30, 2009, 7:36 a.m., https://twitter.com/MuhammadAli/status/1659370445.

6. Ecclesiastes 4:12.

7. Lance Armstrong with Sally Jenkins, *It's Not About the Bike: My Journey Back to Life* (New York: Berkley, 2001), 269.

CHAPTER 11: THE POWER OF YOUR SACRIFICE

1. Robert F. Kennedy, "Day of Affirmation Address, University of Capetown, Capetown, South Africa, June 6, 1966," *John F. Kennedy Presidential Library and Museum*, June 6, 1966, https://www.jfklibrary.org/Research/Research-Aids/Ready-Reference/RFK-Speeches/Day-of-Affirmation-Address-as-delivered.aspx.

2. Nelson Mandela, as quoted in "I Am Prepared to Die": Document Recalls Famous Speech from the Dock," *Nelson Mandela Foundation*, April 20, 2011, https://www.nelsonmandela.org/news/entry/i-am-prepared-to-die.

3. "SA President Nelson Mandela to Step Down," *South African History Online*, March 16, 2011, http://www.sahistory.org.za/dated-event/sa-president-nelson-mandela-step-down.

4. Anup Shah, "Poverty Facts and Stats," *Global Issues*, http://www.globalissues.org/article/26/poverty-facts-and-stats. In this article, poverty is defined as living on less than $2.50 a day.

5. Carol J. Loomis, "Warren Buffett Gives Away His Fortune," *Fortune Magazine: Archives*, June 25, 2006, http://archive.fortune.com/2006/06/25/magazines/fortune/charity1.fortune/index.htm.

6 Loomis, "Warren Buffet Gives Away His Fortune."

7. Luke 21:1-4.

8 "Maximilian Kolbe," Jewish Virtual Library, http://www.jewishvirtuallibrary.org/maximilian-kolbe.

9. David Hudson, "President Obama Awards the Medal of Honor to Sgt. Kyle J. White," *The White House: President Barack Obama*, May 13, 2014, https://obamawhitehouse.archives.gov/blog/2014/05/13/president-obama-awards-medal-honor-sgt-kyle-j-white.

10. "Sergeant Kyle J. White Medal of Honor Operation Enduring Freedom," at https://www.army.mil/medalofhonor/white/battle/index.html#full_narrative.

11. See at http://www.presidency.ucsb.edu/ws/index.php?pid=105185.

12. Kyle J. White, as quoted in David Hudson, "President Obama Awards the Medal of Honor to Sgt. Kyle J. White," *The White House: President Barack Obama*, May 13, 2014, https://obamawhitehouse.archives.gov/blog/2014/05/13/president-obama-awards-medal-honor-sgt-kyle-j-white.

THE POWER OF YOUR ATTITUDE

As much as you try, sometimes you just can't change your circumstances—and never the actions of others. But you do have the power to choose how your attitude affects your outlook on your day and those you influence in your life.

Join Stan Toler as he shares the *what, why,* and *how* behind the transformation you desire. With this book, you'll…

- release the thoughts and habits that keep you from experiencing joy on a daily basis
- learn the seven choices you can make to get out of a rut and into greater success
- implement a plan to improve your outlook in three vital areas and conquer negativity

Having lost his father in an industrial accident as a boy, Toler knows about coping with unexpected tragedies and harsh realities. He will gently guide you through the internal processes that can positively change any life—including yours.

THE POWER OF YOUR BRAIN

Do you find yourself stuck in negative thought patterns? Is your thinking disrupting your day and thwarting your goals?

When you choose to take each thought captive to the obedience of Christ, you drive out the world's way of thinking that breeds depression, discontent, and despair—and make room for more joy, faith, and purpose. Let Stan teach you an easy four-step process for restoring order to your brain:

- *Detoxification*—remove clutter from your mind
- *Realignment*—establish your thoughts on God's truth
- *Reinforcement*—bring others along on the journey
- *Perseverance*—maintain your positive momentum

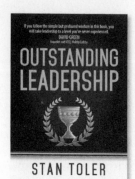

OUTSTANDING LEADERSHIP

What makes a leader stand out? What are the keys to truly making a difference? And how can you become the influencer you were created to be? With more than 40 years of leadership experience, Stan Toler knows what it takes to empower people to reach organizational and personal goals. He cuts through the mystery and confusion and provides clear guidelines to help you accomplish vital leadership tasks, including...

- defining your vision, developing your plan, and communicating clearly to help people buy in to your shared goal

- overcoming common leadership challenges to create a culture of success

- building strong relationships and effective teams that make working hard worthwhile

You'll find all the tools, tips, and practical guidance you need to help individuals and groups reach their highest potential and fulfill their God-given purpose.

MINUTE MOTIVATORS FOR LEADERS

You are a leader—people look to you to be an example, offer direction, and provide inspiration. But with so much to do, how can you keep fresh, focused, and excited about your opportunity to make a difference in people's lives? Stan Toler provides inspirational quotes, one-page gems of wisdom, and memorable taglines to fuel your passion and clarify your vision. You'll find plenty of helpful reminders that...

- Leaders are in the people business. As a leader, your primary function is not to buy, sell, or ply a trade. It is to understand and work with people.

- Bureaucrats run institutions. Leaders lead people. You can make the difference.

- Leadership is a team sport. Do more than direct individuals—build a team.

This treasure of tried-and-true principles will be your on-the-go source for the motivation and encouragement you need to be the effective leader you were created to be.

MINUTE MOTIVATORS FOR WOMEN
STAN TOLER AND LINDA TOLER

Bestselling author Stan Toler and his wife, Linda, share thought-provoking quotes and beautiful words of hope within these pages. Each chapter will draw your attention to a single attribute every godly woman wants to cultivate in her life, such as patience, wisdom, persistence, courage, and gratitude.

Bite-size portions of inspiration make this the perfect devotional for those days when you feel as if you can never get ahead. Recharge in the middle of a hectic schedule or end your day with a much-needed reminder that God has every aspect of your life under control.

MINUTE MOTIVATORS FOR MEN
STAN TOLER

In *Minute Motivators for Men*, Stan Toler offers a playbook for living up to the standard of excellence.

Receive daily guidance on how you can be your best, including how you can take charge by taking control of your attitude, lead with gentle strength wherever you go, and express your feelings—from anger to gratitude—in honest and constructive ways

If you desire to grow in your character and capability, you'll find many powerful and effective tips here. *Minute Motivators for Men* will inspire you to become the leader, husband, father, and friend you've always wanted to be.